PENGUIN BOOKS

MW00681809

WUTHERING HEIGHTS

Dr Stephen Coote was educated at Magdalene College, Cambridge, where he was an Exhibitioner, and at Birkbeck College, University of London, where he was the Senior Research Scholar. He is currently the Advisory Editor of the Penguin Study Notes and Passnotes series, to which he has contributed many studies of works of English literature. Dr Coote has also written on Chaucer and T. S. Eliot for the Penguin Critical Studies series. In addition, he has published a history of medieval English literature and biographies of Byron and William Morris.

Penguin Study Notes

EMILY BRONTË

Wuthering Heights

STEPHEN COOTE, M.A., PH.D.

PENGUIN BOOKS

PENGUIN BOOKS

Published by the Penguin Group
Penguin Books Ltd, 27 Wrights Lane, London W8 5TZ, England
Penguin Putnam Inc., 375 Hudson Street, New York, New York 10014, USA
Penguin Books Australia Ltd, Ringwood, Victoria, Australia
Penguin Books Canada Ltd, 10 Alcorn Avenue, Toronto, Ontario, Canada M4V 3B2
Penguin Books (NZ) Ltd, Private Bag 102902, NSMC Auckland, New Zealand

Penguin Books Ltd, Registered Offices: Harmondsworth, Middlesex, England

First published in Penguin Passnotes 1984
Published in Penguin Study Notes 1999
10 9 8 7 6 5 4 3 2 1

Copyright © Stephen Coote, 1984
All rights reserved

Set in 10/12.5 pt PostScript Monotype Ehrhardt
Typeset by Rowland Phototypesetting Ltd, Bury St Edmunds, Suffolk
Printed in England by Clays Ltd, St Ives plc

Except in the United States of America, this book is sold subject
to the condition that it shall not, by way of trade or otherwise, be lent,
re-sold, hired out, or otherwise circulated without the publisher's
prior consent in any form of binding or cover other than that in
which it is published and without a similar condition including this
condition being imposed on the subsequent purchaser

Contents

To the Student

This book is designed to help you with your studies and examinations. It contains a synopsis of the plot, a glossary of the more unfamiliar words and phrases and a commentary on some of the issues raised by the text. An account of the writer's life is also included for background.

Page references in parentheses refer to the Penguin Classics edition, edited by Pauline Nestor.

When you use this book remember that it is no more than an aid to your study. It will help you find passages quickly and perhaps give you some ideas for essays. But remember: *This book is not a substitute for reading the text and it is your response and your knowledge that matter.* These are the things the examiners are looking for, and they are also the things that will give you the most pleasure. Show your knowledge and appreciation to the examiner, and show them clearly.

Introduction

The Life and Background of Emily Brontë (1818–48)

The life of the Brontës at Haworth is a national legend and their home a place of pilgrimage. Just as *Wuthering Heights* appeals deeply to the imagination, so does the life of its author.

Emily Brontë was the second of three literary sisters. Charlotte, the eldest, gives a fine account of their shared but secretive life of the imagination, a life that found expression in almost continuous literary activity (pp. xxvi–xxxvii). The Brontës began to write in childhood. They created worlds of epic heroes, and so real were these to them that it is easy to see how, as they grew up, these shy, passionate women could give such life to the vivid heroes of their novels.

For recreation the Brontës read books or walked on the moors. Life at the parsonage was not a sociable one. Their mother died in their infancy, and the children were looked after by their aunt. Their father, the curate of Haworth, was a forbidding, distant man.

But this isolated, introverted existence was a seedbed of imagination. The vast energies of the sisters were not squandered on commonplace things. Instead, they were turned inward. Again, just as *Wuthering Heights* itself sets extraordinary events in the most real and detailed settings, so its author nurtured her bizarre imaginings while watching local life and real people with great intensity. Charlotte wrote of her:

My sister's disposition was not naturally gregarious; circumstances favoured and fostered her tendency to seclusion; except to go to church or to take a walk on the hills, she rarely crossed the threshold of home. Though her feeling for the people round was benevolent, intercourse with them she never sought;

nor, with very few exceptions, ever experienced. And yet she knew them; knew their ways, their language, their family histories; she could hear of them with interest and talk of them with detail, minute, graphic and accurate; but *with* them she rarely exchanged a word (pp. xxxiv–xxxv).

Charlotte does not mention their brother, Patrick Branwell Brontë. Branwell was the only son of the family and a young man of great promise. But Branwell was unstable and did not possess his sisters' faculty for channelling his emotions into great art. He could not hold down a job and he fell into debt. He took to drink and became addicted to drugs. His sisters nursed him, but his gloomy presence in the house must go some way to explain Emily's concern, as evinced in her novel, with the ease with which men can reduce themselves to a brutish level. Such melodrama became a part of her daily routine.

With a romantic writer like Emily Brontë it is tempting to explain her novel in terms of her own experiences. Emily Brontë certainly related the events of her own life to *Wuthering Heights*. But her imagination was also fired by her reading: Scott, Byron, Shakespeare. Heathcliff in particular owes something to Byron and Shakespeare, while Scott showed her how to write about wild, primitive people. She also read religious tracts: 'full of miracles and apparitions and preternatural warnings, ominous dreams and frenzied fanaticisms'. These too played their part.

Emily Brontë's is the life of a particular type of artist. She lived passionately in the world of her imagination but never lost her grip on reality. She had a profound knowledge of emotion but as an artist she was never overwhelmed by it. She was never sensational merely for the sake of it.

Why is this? We have not discussed one aspect of Emily's life: her deep moral awareness. It was her father's business, not hers, to preach sermons. Her task in life was to write her novel. But Emily had thought deeply about the nature of love and she designed her novel to show its variety. We should not read *Wuthering Heights* as if it was a diary. It is a novel that is concerned with showing the nature of love. It was, as her sister wrote:

hewn in a wild workshop, with simple tools out of homely materials. The statuary found a granite block on a solitary moor: gazing thereon, he saw how from the crag might be elicited the head, savage, swart, sinister; a form moulded with at least one element of grandeur-power. He wrought with a rude chisel, and from no model but the vision of his meditations. With time and labour, the crag took human shape; and there it stands colossal, dark, and frowning, half statue, half rock; in the former sense, terrible and goblin-like; in the latter, almost beautiful, for its colouring is of mellow grey, and moorland moss clothes it; and heath, with its blooming bells and balmy fragrance, grows faithfully and close to the giant's foot (p. xxxvii).

Emily Brontë's life leads us to her book and it helps to account for many of the things in it, but *Wuthering Heights* is a novel, not an autobiography. It is the only novel of a genius who was dead by the age of thirty.

Synopsis of Wuthering Heights

Mr Lockwood has come to the wilds of Yorkshire to recover from a love affair. He is staying at Thrushcross Grange and goes to nearby Wuthering Heights to meet his landlord. This is the surly, gypsy-like Heathcliff. Lockwood is intrigued by Heathcliff's apparent good breeding, his contempt for the world and his air of suppressed emotion (p. 5). Indeed, so fascinated is Lockwood by Heathcliff that he returns to Wuthering Heights the following day where he is stranded by a snowstorm. On this second visit Lockwood meets two further members of Heathcliff's household: the brutal Hareton Earnshaw and the lovely but off-hand Cathy (pp. 10–18).

The storm obliges Lockwood to remain at Wuthering Heights and he is reluctantly shown a room. Here he sees the names of Catherine Earnshaw, Catherine Heathcliff and Catherine Linton scratched into the paint (p. 19). He also reads the diary of Catherine Earnshaw which she has kept on the blank margins of her books (pp. 20–22). From this Lockwood learns of the relationship between Catherine and Heathcliff and of the unfeeling dogmatism of the servant Joseph's religion. Lockwood then falls asleep but wakes, shouting, from a nightmare. This rouses Heathcliff who orders him from the room; Lockwood leaves but, turning, sees Heathcliff sobbing to the ghost of Catherine Linton, born Catherine Earnshaw (pp. 25–9).

Lockwood returns to Thrushcross Grange. He finds that he has caught a fever. He is nursed by his housekeeper, Nelly Dean, who tells him the story of how Heathcliff became master of both Thrushcross Grange and Wuthering Heights.

*

Lockwood is told that old Mr Earnshaw, the original owner of Wuthering Heights, having gone on business to Liverpool, found an abandoned child (p. 37), whom he brought home and named Heathcliff. The baby was dark skinned, with a hint of the diabolic about him (p. 36). In carrying the boy back, old Mr Earnshaw broke the toys he had bought for his children, Hindley and Catherine. This angered them, and from the start Heathcliff is shown to be both destructive and to breed bad feeling.

Hindley Earnshaw despises Heathcliff but is nonetheless weaker than him (pp. 39–40). Catherine, on the other hand, is drawn to the growing boy, as is her dying father (p. 41). A great childhood friendship develops between Catherine and Heathcliff as they ramble on the moors in defiance of Joseph's dreary religious rules (p. 46).

Eventually old Mr Earnshaw dies (p. 44). Hindley returns for his funeral and, much to everyone's surprise, brings a wife, a sickly and neurotic creature, with him (pp. 45–6). Hindley, as head of the house, gains his revenge on Heathcliff by degrading him to the status of a servant (p. 46). This makes no difference to the growing love between Catherine and Heathcliff: they still roam the moors together, going one day to spy on their neighbours, the Lintons (pp. 48–51). They break into the Lintons' garden and peer into their beautiful house. Such beauty attracts them, but the petulant children, Edgar and Isabella, earn the contempt of both Catherine and Heathcliff.

Heathcliff himself informs Nelly Dean of what they have been doing, for he returns home alone. He and Catherine were caught by the Lintons and severely reprimanded after being chased by the dogs. Catherine had, indeed, been caught and hurt by one of the dogs and she is being nursed in the house by the Lintons. Heathcliff has been told off and sent home. He has noticed that whereas he is treated like a servant, Catherine has been treated as a young lady (p. 51). This social difference between the two will be crucial.

Catherine stays at Thrushcross Grange for five weeks. During this time the tomboy is transformed into a young lady, at least on the surface. A different Catherine returns to Wuthering Heights. Although she asks immediately for Heathcliff and kisses him, the spiteful Hindley has introduced him to her as one of the servants, and after her first

impulsive kiss Catherine laughs at Heathcliff (p. 53). Heathcliff is
mortified. After much thought he decides to try to reform his ways:
he will change from being the wild, unwashed boy. But as Nelly Dean
grooms him she sees how ineradicable are the traces of the dark and
sinister in him (pp. 56–7). Accidentally insulted by Edgar Linton,
Heathcliff retaliates and is severely punished by Hindley, and as Catherine goes to comfort him Heathcliff vows his revenge (p. 60).

Hindley Earnshaw's son is born. This is the brutal Hareton Earnshaw
we met at the start of the novel. Hindley's wife dies in childbirth and
Hindley himself goes into a rapid and degrading decline (p. 65).
Heathcliff, whose sinister nature is beginning to become ever more
clear, watches this decline with some pleasure (p. 65).

Meanwhile, Catherine is growing into an attractive young woman
(p. 65). While she is still attracted to Heathcliff she is also being courted
by Edgar Linton. She begins to take on a 'double character': the natural
Catherine who loves Heathcliff and the young lady who is a suitable
match for Edgar (pp. 66–72). Her double character, it will be seen, is
the basis of her ruin. Her apparent coldness distresses Heathcliff, while
Edgar, although shocked by her extreme behaviour, is in love with
Catherine and confesses his passion after a quarrel with her.

Catherine agrees to marry Edgar but confesses to Nelly Dean that
her soul truly belongs to Heathcliff (pp. 76–82). She says she cannot
marry Heathcliff because he is penniless and such an alliance would
degrade her. Unbeknown to Catherine, Heathcliff has overheard her
conversation with Nelly and he leaves Wuthering Heights (p. 80). In
her great outburst to Nelly Dean we see the depth and elemental force
contained in Catherine's love for Heathcliff. By denying these she has
denied her soul. In her agony and confusion she runs out into a storm
and catches a fever.

Catherine marries Edgar Linton three years later. The marriage is a
fairly good one, untroubled until Heathcliff returns (pp. 91–2). This,
of course, he does (p. 92) and the love denied three years earlier begins
to take its terrible revenge.

Heathcliff returns a wealthy man, but despite his appearance of
gentility, his eyes are still full of the 'black fire' of his youth (p. 95).

He wants to murder Edgar and we discover that he has taken lodgings with his old, depraved enemy Hindley Earnshaw. Heathcliff is working on the further destruction of him and his son.

At Heathcliff's return, Catherine is thrown into frenzied excitement (p. 94). The wild, elemental love in her has been revived, but the continued suppression of this love will wreak ruin and eventually kill her. Isabella Linton, Edgar's sister, also falls passionately in love with Heathcliff (pp. 99–106). He is indifferent to her but uses her infatuation to gain her hand in marriage and thus, if Edgar has no male heirs, possession of Thrushcross Grange.

Confrontations between Heathcliff and Edgar show Edgar to be by far the weaker man (pp. 112–115). The strain of this brings Catherine to the point of breakdown. She becomes ill and delirious and longs for death (pp. 119–25).

Heathcliff runs away with Isabella who is disowned by Edgar (pp. 129–31). Edgar exhausts himself looking after the dying Catherine. Heathcliff's evil intentions are now clear. He intends to ruin Hindley, Hareton and Isabella and the marriage of Edgar and Catherine. Nonetheless, if he is evil he is also profoundly romantic. He is deeply in love with Catherine and is tormented by his love. The fact that she is dying is almost unbearable to him (p. 158). He then confesses his love and rounds on her for denying them both happiness (pp. 160–61). The strain becomes intolerable for Catherine. Heathcliff is thrown into a despair that is both primeval and animal-like (pp. 165–7). On her deathbed Catherine gives birth to a daughter (p. 164).

Isabella has run away from Heathcliff soon after their wretched marriage (pp. 134–143 and 169–82). She has watched Heathcliff destroying Hindley; she goes to London and is not heard of again until her death, when she leaves behind her a child, Heathcliff's son Linton.

Heathcliff wins the whole of Wuthering Heights whilst gambling with Hindley. Hareton Earnshaw, the rightful owner of Wuthering Heights, is now a penniless brute. Heathcliff is grimly satisfied with his victory (pp. 185–6).

Catherine's child, the young Cathy, grows up. She is a lively and attractive girl, a milder version of her mother (p. 187). She is not allowed out of the grounds of Thrushcross Grange where she stays until Edgar, her father, goes to London to sort out his dead sister's affairs. When she does go out she inevitably finds her way to Wuthering Heights where she meets Hareton Earnshaw. She is repelled by him (pp. 192–4).

Edgar returns from London with the sickly Linton Heathcliff whose father at once claims him (pp. 197–201). The boy does not meet Cathy again until her sixteenth birthday when, roaming the moors, she meets Heathcliff who invites her to Wuthering Heights (p. 212). Cathy and Linton become fond of each other, but we see the spiteful Linton taunting Hareton and showing his peevish sickliness (p. 218). Cathy and Linton exchange love letters until this is stopped by Nelly Dean (pp. 222–5).

Saddened by the thought of her father's imminent death and the ending of her love affair with Linton, Cathy walks on the moors. She encounters Heathcliff who informs her that Linton is dying for her love (pp. 230–31). Fascinated by this, and despite her father's injunction not to go to Wuthering Heights, Cathy persuades Nelly Dean to visit with her. Their love is revived at this meeting despite Linton's erratic behaviour (pp. 234–41).

During Nelly's ensuing three-week illness, Cathy rides over to see Linton nearly every day (p. 244). But, if Linton has been forced to love Cathy largely by his father so that Heathcliff can be doubly sure of securing Thrushcross Grange, Hareton Earnshaw has genuinely fallen in love with her. He tries to learn to read and to improve himself but Cathy remains contemptuous and cruel towards him (pp. 246–8).

The dying Edgar, hoping that Cathy may at least have some share in Thrushcross Grange, allows occasional meetings between Cathy and Linton (p. 256). The boy is also now clearly dying and is forced by his father to beg that Cathy and Nelly Dean return with him to Wuthering Heights (p. 266). They agree to do so and are made Heathcliff's prisoners. He forces the marriage between Cathy and his son (see p. 72 of this book).

Edgar is mortified at this but is unable to change his will against Heathcliff's favour (pp. 279–81). His dying consolation is that Cathy manages to escape to tend his last hours (p. 280). She is pursued by Heathcliff, rounds on him, but accompanies him back to Wuthering

Heights where Linton eventually dies. That joyless period of her life begins in which we see her at the start of the novel.

Heathcliff now confesses to Nelly Dean the depth and anguish of his love for Catherine (pp. 285–8). He lives in an abyss of hell without her. He has even tried to dig up her grave, and for eighteen years has been haunted by her ghost. He has bribed the sexton to remove the side of Catherine's coffin and has secured his promise to do the same to his. The lovers will lie together in death as they never could in life.

At this point the story is deadlocked. Lockwood decides to return to London, ignoring Nelly Dean's suggestion that he should marry Cathy to save her from her wretched existence (p. 295).

By chance, Lockwood returns the following year. Heathcliff has died and Hareton, Cathy and Nelly Dean are all living in a calmer and happier Wuthering Heights. Lockwood sees Cathy teaching Hareton to read and is aware of the love that has grown between them (pp. 304–5).

Nelly Dean describes the growth of their love, a love stronger than the power of Heathcliff's hatred. She describes how Heathcliff weakened as he approached death (pp. 319–21). The young people begin to stand up to him and he lacks the power to destroy them (pp. 315–18). They both remind him too much of Catherine with whom he longs to be united (p. 319–21). He eventually dies in a state of both elation and great spiritual pain (pp. 324–32). The hatred and desire for revenge that his thwarted love has inspired are shown to be weaker than true love. The two families he tried to break and ruin are to be united in marriage (p. 333). Despite Lockwood's sonorous and powerful meditation on the dead lovers' peace (p. 334), Heathcliff's ghost is said by some to haunt the neighbourhood (p. 333).

An Account of the Plot

Emily Brontë does not tell her story in a simple way. She does not start at the beginning and take us straight through to the end. Instead, she begins almost at the climax of her tale. Why? Because she wants to build up an atmosphere of mystery and suspense. She wants to awaken our curiosity about her strange, unfriendly characters. Only when we have been introduced to them can she allow Nelly Dean to explain why they are so bitter.

VOLUME I

Chapter 1, *pp. 3–8*

Mr Lockwood introduces himself to us. We learn that he is recovering from a mild but unhappy love affair and has come to the Yorkshire moors, to this 'perfect misanthropist's Heaven', to recuperate. The strangeness and isolation at first appeal to his weak nature, while his timid love affair (p. 6) is in strong contrast to the grand passions of the novel.

Lockwood explains the meaning of the word 'Wuthering' as 'descriptive of . . . atmospheric tumult . . . in stormy weather'. Throughout the novel the violence and grandeur of the weather over the bleak moors will accompany the passions of those who live there. Indeed, they will be a part of them.

Lockwood then describes in detail the rough, practical farmhouse called Wuthering Heights and introduces us to its owner, Heathcliff: 'He is a dark skinned gypsy, in aspect, in dress, and manners a gentleman, that is, as much a gentleman as many a country squire.' We see at once two crucial and contradictory aspects of Heathcliff's character: his romantic, gypsy strangeness and his seeming gentlemanly ways. Lockwood immediately adds a third characteristic: the suppressed passion under his grim exterior. *Wuthering Heights* will be largely concerned with Heathcliff's feelings, with his strangeness, his love and the results of the bitter frustration that have made him master of both Thrushcross Grange and of Wuthering Heights itself.

Heathcliff makes an effort to be civil but the boorish behaviour of the servant Joseph and, even more, the aggressiveness of the dogs, convey the brutal and hostile atmosphere in which Heathcliff is master. We can be sure that his hatred of the world is more passionate and sincere than Lockwood's.

Lockwood returns to Thrushcross Grange.

Chapter 2, *pp. 9–18*

Lockwood goes back to Wuthering Heights, arriving there just before a snowstorm. This symbol of the weather will be used in Chapter 3 for one of Emily Brontë's most startling effects. Lockwood now meets Hareton Earnshaw and the younger Catherine. The latter is physically very attractive (p. 11) but this beauty is in marked contrast to her off-hand behaviour to her guest. Lockwood tries to be polite. He thinks that Cathy is Heathcliff's wife, a cruel irony we only appreciate when we learn that young Catherine is the daughter of the woman Heathcliff has loved, another Catherine.

Hareton Earnshaw is seen to be virtually a brute. The description on pp. 11–12 makes this clear and introduces us to the theme of moral and physical degradation which is so important in this book. We also should remember that it is these two young people, Cathy and Hareton, who will be redeemed by their love at the end of the novel.

When Heathcliff enters he informs Lockwood that Cathy is not his wife but his daughter-in-law. Lockwood jumps to the conclusion that Hareton is Heathcliff's son. He is wrong again. Lockwood is bluntly told that Cathy's husband is dead.

You should not worry if the relationships seem so complicated at this point. We share Lockwood's confusion. We are also given a clue as to how complicated and closeknit the true relationships in the book are.

Lockwood is now trapped at the house by the snowstorm and the hostile inhabitants of Wuthering Heights are rudely indifferent to his discomfort, a mood intensified by Heathcliff himself. Eventually Lockwood seizes Joseph's lantern and rushes out, only to be brought down by the dogs. The dogs draw blood and Zillah, the housekeeper, throws water over Lockwood to revive him. He is dragged back into the house and reluctantly given a bed for the night.

The physical violence of the scene sets the atmosphere of hatred exactly and forms an excellent contrast to the emotional agonies of the next chapter.

Chapter 3, *pp. 19–32*

This chapter is one of Emily Brontë's finest and you should think carefully about the issues it raises.

Lockwood is taken to a bedroom about which he is asked to keep silent. He asks why and is told that in it have been 'many queer goings on'. Left alone Lockwood discovers mildewed books on a ledge and three names scratched in the paint: Catherine Earnshaw, Catherine Heathcliff, Catherine Linton. Just as these names echo in the sleeping Lockwood's head, so they will throughout the book.

Awake again after fitful sleep, Lockwood begins to read the Bible of Catherine Earnshaw. She, of course, is the mother of the Cathy whom we have already met. From his reading Lockwood learns that this Catherine has a married brother called Hindley who is indifferent to the sufferings that Catherine and Heathcliff endure under Joseph. Joseph is pictured as a religious bigot, an impression which is confirmed in Chapter 5 when Nelly Dean describes him as: 'the wearisomest, self-righteous pharisee that ever ransacked a Bible to rake the promises to himself, and fling the curses on his neighbours.' Their suffering clearly brings the children together, and this is the first we learn of the childhood relationship between Heathcliff and Catherine. It is a relationship clearly established in defiance of authority by two high-spirited children.

A revolt against Joseph and its punishment are mentioned.

Falling asleep again, Lockwood begins to dream, this time of a wearisome sermon on sin. He wakes to find the dream has been suggested by no more than a branch tapping against the window. Falling asleep and dreaming once more Lockwood believes that this time he sees the ghost of Catherine herself, the Catherine who owned the Bible and who now calls herself Catherine Linton. Only later, when Catherine Earnshaw does indeed become Catherine Linton, shall we see how portentous Lockwood's dream has been. So horrible is the dream, however, that he cries out and rouses Heathcliff who orders him from the room. Heathcliff is violently angered by the mention of Catherine's name.

Lockwood leaves the room, as he is asked to. Pausing a moment in the dark passage, he sees Heathcliff throw himself on to the bed and call out to the ghost of Catherine in utter anguish (p. 28–9). Nothing could make clearer the intensity of the relationship between Heathcliff and Catherine or show more completely the depths of Heathcliff's suppressed emotions.

What has Emily Brontë done here? In this single chapter she has given us a foretaste of the whole book: the hostility of Wuthering Heights, the violence of the natural world and the overwhelming nature of passion are all shown to us. In addition, by having the scenes observed through the eyes of a man whose nerves are heightened by fever, who sleeps fitfully and nervously, she has made her presentation as extreme as possible. All involved experience great moral and physical discomfort; and the events in real life are scarcely less bizarre than those in the dreams. In her description of this emotional chaos Emily Brontë shows the intense, irrational and nightmarish quality of Heathcliff and Catherine's passion. We are prepared for a love story that will deeply probe emotion and melodrama.

In the morning Lockwood goes away, losing himself in the snowdrifts before he finally returns, exhausted, to Thrushcross Grange.

Chapter 4, *pp. 33–40*

The main part of the novel begins here with the start of Nelly Dean's narrative, told to the ailing Lockwood.

Nelly Dean informs Lockwood that Heathcliff is now a rich man and then explains the complicated family relationship. There are two families: the Earnshaws and the Lintons. Their connections are set out in the family tree below.

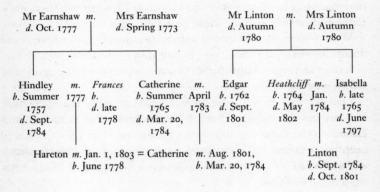

What we want to know is how Heathcliff has intruded into this circle.

Mrs Dean tells us. Heathcliff is a foundling. Old Mr Earnshaw goes to Liverpool one day, promising to return with a fiddle for Hindley and whip for Catherine. He returns instead with Heathcliff. In the effort of carrying him home, old Earnshaw breaks the fiddle and loses the whip. The children blame Heathcliff for this and hate him. Heathcliff himself is described as a 'gypsy brat' and a child 'as dark as almost as if it came from the devil'. Heathcliff's destructiveness, his gypsy birth and the suggestion of the devil about him will all be developed in the novel. As Mrs Dean says: 'from the very beginning, he bred bad feeling in the house.'

Though Catherine grows fond of Heathcliff, the child is bullied by the family: even Mrs Dean cannot warm to him. Heathcliff is surly but does not complain about his treatment. But the incident with the horse at the end of the chapter shows that Heathcliff can get his own way when he wants to, and exposes his lack of resentment at his treatment as being only superficial.

Chapter 5, *pp. 41–4*

Old Mr Earnshaw is dying. As his body weakens, so do his mind and sensibilities. (We should note the strong theme of mental and physical decay in *Wuthering Heights*.) He begins to dote on Heathcliff, valuing him more highly than his own son, a weakness which will be a great cause of trouble later in the book.

We are becoming more aware of the growing power of Joseph and his dreary religious views.

In this chapter we also begin to see the children growing up and note the ties of feeling between them. Catherine is high spirited: there is an important description of her near the start of the chapter (p. 42). We see here also how her fondness for Heathcliff has flourished. Mrs Dean says: 'The greatest punishment we could invent for her was to keep her separate from him: yet she got chided more than any of us on his account.' Thus a certain recklessness is clear in Catherine, especially where Heathcliff is concerned. He, for his part, 'Would do *her* bidding in anything'; the signs of a passionate lover are clear even in Heathcliff the boy. Finally, old Earnshaw dies and when Catherine, who discovers this, turns to Heathcliff for comfort, it is an indication of where her feelings lie at this moment of crisis.

The chapter ends with one of the very rare idyllic scenes of Heathcliff and Catherine together. Again, it shows the natural and spontaneous depth of their feelings for each other.

Chapter 6, *pp. 45–51*

Hindley, who has been away for three years, returns home for his father's funeral bringing, much to everyone's surprise, a wife. She is a sickly, neurotic creature. In his jealousy, Hindley banishes Heathcliff to the servants' quarters.

The love between the growing Catherine and Heathcliff continues, despite the fact that Heathcliff has now been relegated to the status of a servant by his jealous adopted brother and his wife. In an important passage, Emily Brontë shows the healthy, defiant extroversion of the children's feelings: '. . . it was one of their chief amusements to run away to the moors in the morning and remain there all day, and the after punishment grew a mere thing to laugh at.' Again there is a slight suggestion of the wrongfulness of their friendship.

One day they go off together and Heathcliff returns alone. He explains to Nelly Dean that he and Catherine have been to Thrushcross Grange to spy on the Lintons. Heathcliff had wanted to know if they spent their Sundays as he and Catherine are forced to, listening to the dreary sermons of Joseph.

Heathcliff describes (p. 48) what he and Catherine have seen: it is a picture at once sophisticated, beautiful and unnatural. Thrushcross Grange is a contrast to Wuthering Heights: it is a luxurious place where the two children 'should have thought themselves in heaven'. But the two children inside, Edgar and Isabella Linton, are markedly different to the Heathcliff and Catherine who peer in through the window. They are spoiled and highly strung, and from the start earn Heathcliff's contempt. There is nothing natural about them and Heathcliff and Catherine 'made frightful noises to terrify them yet more'.

This brings Catherine and Heathcliff to the attention of Mr and Mrs Linton who are shocked by their behaviour; Heathcliff is sent away in disgrace, but Catherine, who has been attacked by one of the dogs, is ordered to stay behind.

As he recounts the incident to Nelly Dean, Heathcliff's love for Catherine is more obvious than ever before (p. 51). He describes the beauty of her hair and her obvious superiority to the Linton children. But he is also aware of something else: the cruel and absolute divisions of class which he and Catherine have disregarded at Wuthering Heights. 'She was a young lady,' he says of Catherine, 'and they made a distinction between her treatment and mine.'

This scene is of great importance to the whole of the novel. We are introduced to the Lintons just as we see Catherine's and Heathcliff's friendship ripening into young love. That which will help to destroy them is present almost at the start of their mature feelings. Sophistication and an awareness of social class which are far from healthy have intruded into the novel. They have also intruded into the love of Catherine and Heathcliff to wreck it and help work out its tragic consequences.

Chapter 7, *pp. 52–62*

Catherine stays at Thrushcross Grange for five weeks. During this time she is turned into a young lady. When she returns to her home she is seen as more accomplished than Isabella Linton but we see also that she is more full-blooded than Isabella. She asks almost at once for Heathcliff.

Heathcliff is still the unwashed, uncultivated boy he was when we last saw him. Hindley takes a spiteful delight in introducing him to Catherine 'like the other servants'. The new, sophisticated Catherine laughs at Heathcliff and hurts him deeply. He dashes out of the room. Mrs Linton requests that her own children 'be kept carefully away from that naughty, swearing boy'.

After much thought Heathcliff comes to Nelly Dean and asks her to make him decent: 'I'm going to be good.' He realizes that his boorish behaviour has hurt Catherine, but as Nelly Dean begins to encourage him (p. 56) we see that the traces of 'black fiends' and the 'devil's spies' are indelibly marked on Heathcliff's face.

As Nelly is attending to Heathcliff's appearance, Edgar Linton comes in. He unintentionally insults Heathcliff who empties a tureen of hot apple sauce over him. Heathcliff's animal vitality is not easily subdued but in contrast we see that Edgar Linton is a wretchedly soft and nervy little boy, whose cries bring the rest of the household to the kitchen. Catherine stands up for Heathcliff but Heathcliff is beaten and Catherine suffers for him. She cannot eat and creeps up later to the attic where Heathcliff has been confined. He swears his revenge: 'I'm trying to settle how I shall pay Hindley back. I don't care how long I wait, if only I can do it, at last. I hope he will not die before I do!' This sounds no more than hurt childish pride, but it is the moment at which Heathcliff's long nurtured resentment begins to work itself out.

Chapter 8, *pp. 63–72*

Nelly Dean's story moves on to the next summer. Hindley Earnshaw's child is born. This, of course, is the brutal Hareton Earnshaw we met at the start of the book. The child's mother dies soon after the birth, and with extraordinary suddenness Hindley goes into a moral and physical decline (p. 65). Such swift decline is a feature of this novel and a part of Emily Brontë's concern with the effects of extreme emotions. Heathcliff watches Hindley's deterioration with undisguised pleasure. As Mrs Dean says, the diabolic is becoming increasingly clear in his character. Hatred has begun to play a stronger part than ever in his feelings.

Catherine is now growing into a beautiful woman: high-spirited, arrogant, but for all that with 'a wondrous constancy to old attachments'. Heathcliff and Edgar Linton both interest her and she takes on what Nelly Dean significantly calls a 'double character'. Her divided feelings between the passionate, natural Heathcliff on the one hand and the cultivated and rather delicate Edgar on the other will have tragic consequences. For the moment we see her caught between the two (p. 66).

Depressed at losing Catherine's sole attention, Heathcliff contrives to see her, but Catherine is dressed to meet Edgar. We are told at once how boorish Heathcliff has become (p. 67). Again we see how easily the characters in the book decline from even the slightest degree of cultivation.

Heathcliff compares the number of times Catherine has seen him with the number of times she has seen Edgar. She tells him he is dull company: this mortifies him. At this moment Edgar comes in. Emily Brontë draws a sharp distinction between him and Heathcliff, evoking imagery of the landscape in her comparison of the two (p. 69).

Catherine is clearly over-excited and she turns on Nelly who has been ordered to chaperone her and Edgar. She pinches Nelly hard and then denies touching her. Nelly shows her her arm and Edgar sees Catherine strike her. He is appalled. Trying to rescue Hareton from her he is struck in his turn. He tries to leave but does not get very far before he is called back. Nelly realizes that he is quite powerless. It is his fate to love Catherine. A little while later the two young people confess their love for each other.

Chapter 9, *pp. 73–89*

The opening of this chapter presents us with the physical and mental decline of Hindley. He is now drinking to excess and almost kills his son, Hareton, who is saved, ironically, through the intervention of Heathcliff. The violence and melodrama of this scene remind us forcibly of how close the characters in the novel live to raw emotion.

It is in this chapter too that events take a decisive turn for Heathcliff, Catherine and Edgar.

Catherine is now twenty-two. Edgar has asked her to marry him and she tells Nelly that she has agreed to accept his proposal.

Nelly, always the personification of kind though not always gentle commonsense, asks Catherine her reasons for accepting. She gives these (p. 77–8) and they are, of course, inadequate. Catherine knows this deep down: 'In whichever place the soul lives – in my soul, and in my heart, I'm convinced I'm wrong!' Her passionate nature and the radical honesty of her extreme emotion rise to the surface. Catherine's dreams, her whole being, tie her to the earth rather than to the heavens, to the moors and, above all, to Heathcliff. Her outburst on p. 80 makes this abundantly clear. Her love for Heathcliff has never been more explicit. Their souls are linked by all they have shared, and she confesses 'he's more myself than I am'. The gentle somewhat delicate Edgar is a mere moonbeam compared to Heathcliff's lightning. The difference between the two men could not be more marked.

Heathcliff has overheard all this. He has also, quite unbeknown to her, for the kitchen is dark, heard Catherine say that it would degrade her to marry him. It is enough. He steals out. The social division, made clear when he and Catherine first glimpsed the Linton children, has now asserted itself to destroy all traces of hopeful love. All that remains to Heathcliff are obsession and revenge.

It is perhaps the cruellest irony in the novel that Heathcliff leaves at this point. He fails to hear the rest of Catherine's declaration, fails to hear her great outburst (middle of the chapter, p. 82) in which she declares that by marrying Edgar she will be able to help him, and, more important:

My love for Linton is like the foliage in the woods. Time will change it, I'm well aware, as winter changes the trees. My love for Heathcliff resembles the eternal rocks beneath – a source of little visible delight, but necessary. Nelly, I *am* Heathcliff – he's always, always in my mind – not as a pleasure, any more than I am always a pleasure to myself – but as my own being . . .

This is one of Emily Brontë's most passionate statements on the nature of love and it is worth considering carefully. She does not show love as a sweet, softly sentimental delight. It can be painful and unpleasant, an obsession as fundamental as the bones of the landscape in which her characters live. Above all, perhaps, love is the sense of losing oneself in the other person. Catherine's whole being centres on Heathcliff, and we are shown right at the start of the novel the degree of Heathcliff's identification with her. When thwarted, this sort of love can only have a tragic outcome.

Catherine runs out to find Heathcliff but he, of course, has gone. A titanic storm breaks over the moors. This is nature's equivalent of the emotional outburst we have just witnessed. Catherine gets thoroughly drenched and when she finally returns home she is sick with fever. (See the note on the 'pathetic fallacy' on p. 70 of this book.)

Unlike Mr and Mrs Linton who die after being caught in the rain, Catherine recovers. Three years later Catherine and Edgar Linton are married. Nelly Dean and the couple move to Thrushcross Grange.

Chapter 10, *pp. 90–106*

During his continued illness Nelly Dean relates her story to Lockwood.

She and Catherine then move to Thrushcross Grange with Edgar. Both the marriage and the couple's relation to Isabella, Edgar's sister, seem highly satisfactory. Nonetheless, Edgar is aware of Catherine's excitable and difficult nature. Catherine's depressions are ascribed to her recent illness but they clearly have an emotional origin too.

Heathcliff suddenly returns, a rich and respectable man. All chance of happiness is gone, for the depths of his own emotions are still clear (p. 93) and the effect of his return is to throw Catherine into the wildest excitement. She still loves Heathcliff passionately but Edgar's reaction, not unnaturally, is one of disdain. He still thinks of Heathcliff as a servant for he has not yet seen Heathcliff's partial transformation into a gentleman. Nonetheless, wealthy though Heathcliff has become, 'a half-civilized ferocity lurked yet in the depressed brows, and the eyes full of black fire' (p. 95). Heathcliff has advanced socially but the old, natural passion within him cannot be obscured. His murderous feelings towards Edgar are barely suppressed.

We learn that Heathcliff has taken lodgings with Hindley Earnshaw in Wuthering Heights. This surprising arrangement is apparently made so that he can come to see Catherine more easily. But we should be suspicious of these overtures to Heathcliff's oldest and bitterest enemy.

Isabella Linton, Edgar's sister, falls hopelessly in love with the new Heathcliff. She is only eighteen. Edgar, knowing well Heathcliff's true nature, is horrified. Heathcliff is wholly indifferent to Isabella, but Edgar believes that he intentionally encouraged her to fall in love with him. Their marriage will be part of Heathcliff's revenge. Through Isabella he will get Thrushcross Grange (see p. 72 of this book).

Catherine is appalled at the thought of Isabella loving Heathcliff. She knows too well exactly what sort of man he is and she realizes that Isabella cannot comprehend him at all. She gives a picture of Heathcliff (pp. 101–2) which is far from the conventional one of a lover. She emphasizes Heathcliff's untamed wildness, his total lack of civilized morals. Only a woman like Catherine herself could truly love him.

We learn that Hindley is gambling heavily with Heathcliff whom we see treating Isabella with cruel indifference. Nonetheless, Isabella is Edgar's heir unless he and Catherine have children. With this in mind Heathcliff meditates his revenge. What he suffered as a boy he will make good as a man.

Chapter 11, *pp. 107–18*

Nelly Dean has an irresistible desire to pay a visit to Wuthering Heights, where she encounters Hindley's son, Hareton. But Heathcliff, of whom we are now profoundly suspicious, is working on the boy's mental and moral ruin. The devil in him has gained the upper hand. Nelly Dean feels 'as scared as if I had raised a goblin'.

At his next meeting with Catherine, Heathcliff is told that if he quarrels with Edgar and deceives Isabella into thinking he loves her then he will indeed have his revenge on Catherine (p. 112). Heathcliff meditates on this. When Edgar returns he tries to order Heathcliff from the house. Weak though he is, Edgar recognizes the claims of moral decency and is fully aware of the sort of man Heathcliff is (p. 113). He wants to protect himself.

Edgar realizes he is weaker than Heathcliff and calls his servants. Catherine is dismayed by Edgar's cowardice. Heathcliff smashes his way out of the house to safety.

The strain of these events, of her irresistible attraction to Heathcliff and her loyalty to her husband, brings Catherine to the point of breakdown. Her marriage, even her life, are threatened. Her passionate nature is revolted by Edgar's cold decency and moral firmness. He, for his part, sulks in his library. Heathcliff's presence has destroyed his marriage.

Chapter 12, *pp. 119–31*

Catherine is now delirious. Hatred and mutual suspicion rule at Thrushcross Grange. Wavering between delusion and despair, Catherine gives a vivid picture of her ruined life (pp. 123–5). She longs for the openness of the moors. When Edgar finally comes in to see her her thoughts have turned to death (p. 126). Exhausted and all but broken, Catherine is living on another plane.

Nelly Dean goes to fetch the doctor, and on her way she discovers, to her astonishment and wonder, Isabella's dog, almost strangled. The doctor has heard of Heathcliff's plan to run off with Isabella. Nelly Dean rushes back to Thrushcross Grange only to find that the abduction has already taken place.

The distraught Edgar disowns his sister.

Chapter 13, *pp. 132–43*

Edgar exhausts himself looking after the fading Catherine. Nelly Dean receives a letter from Isabella.

Within twenty-four hours Isabella is bitterly repenting her love affair with Heathcliff. She wonders if he is mad or if he is the devil himself (p. 134). She longs to return to Thrushcross Grange, but Edgar will not take her back.

We see now how much destruction Heathcliff has wrought on the inhabitants of Wuthering Heights: Hindley, Hareton and Isabella herself. The depraved and desperate Hindley wants to murder Heathcliff.

The effects of his evil are now abundantly clear.

Chapter 14, *pp. 144–52*

Edgar is shown Isabella's letter but cannot bring himself to forgive her. Nelly Dean goes to Wuthering Heights with his reply.

Here she encounters Heathcliff, and Emily Brontë provides us with an important insight into the nature of Heathcliff's passion. In the last chapter the reader learned to hate him. While this feeling is not altogether changed, it is modified as he explains the nature of his love to Nelly Dean (pp. 146–7).

The force of Heathcliff's love makes its own rules and brings with it its own morality. It is not the decent, commonplace morality of Edgar which Heathcliff utterly despises: 'But do you imagine that I shall leave Catherine to his *duty* and *humanity*? and can you compare my feelings respecting Catherine, to his?' We have seen already that Catherine compares Heathcliff to lightning and Edgar to a moonbeam. Both Heathcliff and Catherine are aware that his virile force must be exerted and respected. Heathcliff declares that had he been in Edgar's place he would have respected such passion as his and taken revenge only when it had passed. In his speech (p. 147) Heathcliff gives a powerful, contemptuous assessment of Edgar's passion. In the strength of his own feeling that comes over so clearly, we too are forced to recognize that there is something elemental about Heathcliff's love. It is a force as basic as a storm in the natural world. It is also pitiless. We may be repelled by Heathcliff but we are bound also to stand in awe of him.

His treatment of Isabella remains abominable. Heathcliff is a soul in pain and, like Satan, it is his hatred that gives him strength and the will to live (p. 150).

He vows to continue to haunt Thrushcross Grange, a gesture at once profoundly romantic and threatening.

He persuades Nelly Dean to take a letter to Catherine.

VOLUME II

Chapter 1, *pp. 155–63*

This chapter describes the last earthly meeting between Heathcliff and Catherine. The romanticism of the whole novel reaches a new height: passionate love and the approach of death mingle in profound pathos.

Nelly Dean has just delivered Heathcliff's letter when he himself arrives at Thrushcross Grange. The Catherine he encounters is calm but her appearance has altered: 'there seemed unearthly beauty in the change.'

Heathcliff recognizes immediately that she is dying and he is thrown into despair. Catherine declares that it is he (and Edgar) who has killed her. Unearthly though the change in her appearance is, she has lost none of her cruelty and Nelly Dean describes her face and 'the wild vindictiveness in its white cheek'. Catherine tortures Heathcliff with accusations of future unfaithfulness and of forgetting her: Despite everything, we sympathize deeply with Heathcliff (p. 159) as he declares that her words will be branded on him forever.

Her fit subsiding, Catherine says she will suffer even after her death for whatever pain she has inflicted on Heathcliff.

It is interesting to compare this statement to the final paragraph of the novel and to try to decide whether Lockwood's optimism is really justified.

Heathcliff is unable to speak for sheer emotion and Catherine begins to rejoice in the peace that death will bring her. The couple fly to each other in passionate embrace. Heathcliff's outburst here (pp. 160–61) is of the greatest importance. Try to learn the passage (last paragraph) by heart, for nearly the whole novel is concentrated in it.

In this speech Heathcliff upbraids Catherine for her cruelty and, more important, for her betrayal of their love. By denying that love and by stifling her emotions she has killed herself. By the cruellest of ironies, it is only Catherine who could have destroyed such passion:

Because misery, and degradation, and death, and nothing that God or satan could inflict would have parted us, *you*, of your own will, did it. I have not broken your heart – *you* have broken it – and in breaking it, you have broken mine.

Here lies the profound and tragic paradox of the novel. Unable to accept Heathcliff for social reasons, Catherine has not saved herself at all. She has denied the elemental force of love, both her love and Heathcliff's. In so doing she has destroyed both of them. But she, at least, can escape in death. Heathcliff must live on as much a ghost as a man, tortured forever by his frustration. The massive passion roused in him will be wholly perverted and turn to hatred. The remainder of the novel – indeed, the second half of it – will be concerned with the nature of this evil.

Edgar returns. He has been in church while this scene takes place.

Catherine faints and Heathcliff hands her to her husband. Nelly Dean asks Heathcliff to leave; he does so but declares he will wait in the garden.

Chapter 2, *pp. 164–8*

Catherine dies giving birth to the young Cathy we met in the second chapter.

Nelly Dean goes to tell the waiting Heathcliff of Catherine's death. She tells him she died at peace. He, in the madness of his grief, calls Catherine a liar for not remembering him at her end (p. 167). Just as Catherine confessed that Heathcliff was her whole being, so Heathcliff now confesses that she was his. Life is an unbearable abyss without her and he begs that he may be haunted by Catherine so that he can live. The pathetic, primeval animal in Heathcliff comes poignantly to the surface: 'He dashed his head against the knotted trunk; and, lifting up his eyes, howled, not like a man, but like a savage beast getting goaded to death with knives and spears.'

Catherine is buried. Significantly, her grave lies at the edge of the churchyard, in a corner where the moor (the symbol of her passionate nature) has begun to invade.

Chapter 3, *pp. 169–86*

Isabella runs away from Wuthering Heights, unable to tolerate her life there any longer. She throws her wedding ring into the fire. She sees Heathcliff as no more than a monster and she calls Catherine's love for him depraved. She witnesses Hindley's attempt to murder Heathcliff. This is foiled and Heathcliff kicks him and dashes his head against the flagstones.

Isabella goes to London and is never seen again.

Mrs Dean now compares the effect of the deaths of their wives on Edgar and Hindley: time brings Edgar resignation, Hindley is only plunged into deeper despair. Nelly Dean ascribes Edgar's greater happiness to his Christian fortitude. The theme of happiness based on love and virtue begins to resound.

When Hindley dies, the entire Wuthering Heights estate has been mortgaged to Heathcliff. Hareton Earnshaw, the rightful heir, is left to penury and depravity. Heathcliff expresses a 'flinty gratification' at his victory.

Chapter 4, *pp. 187–96*

Nelly Dean describes the childhood of young Cathy. She is as beautiful as, but milder than, her mother and not entirely lacking in spirit. The girl is kept within the bounds of Thrushcross Grange. News of Isabella's death reaches Edgar who goes to London to sort out her affairs.

During her father's absence Cathy fulfils her wish and wanders out of the grounds of Thrushcross Grange. She finds her way to Wuthering Heights. Here she is seen chatting to the eighteen-year-old Hareton.

Cathy is reluctant to leave and tactlessly questions Hareton about the ownership of Wuthering Heights. To her horror she learns that Hareton is her cousin. Nelly Dean examines the young man carefully. Despite his uncouth appearance and behaviour, she believes she can detect better things in him than at first appear. She realizes that Heathcliff has 'bent his malevolence on making him a brute'. Only Joseph, who cares little enough for him, makes Hareton proud of his family name.

The effects of Heathcliff's evil and the very remote possibility of redemption are suggested.

Cathy promises not to tell her father she has visited Wuthering Heights.

Chapter 5, *pp. 197–201*

Isabella has died. Edgar returns with her son, Linton Heathcliff. Nelly Dean describes him as 'a pale, delicate, effeminate boy, who might have been taken for my master's younger brother, so strong was the

resemblance; but there was a sickly peevishness in his aspect, that
Edgar Linton never had'.

The themes of weakness and extreme nervousness are again clear.
Heathcliff's son has nothing of his own passion. He will become
Heathcliff's tool. Heathcliff at once sends Joseph to fetch the boy, but
Edgar refuses to let him go until he has rested for the night.

Chapter 6, *pp. 202–8*

To prevent Heathcliff from coming to Thrushcross Grange Linton is
taken to Wuthering Heights by Nelly Dean.

The child is dismayed at the sight of his unknown father whom he
meets on the way. Heathcliff has come to claim his 'property' whom
he sees for the first time. He regards Linton with utter contempt.
However, he is his heir and in the absence of Edgar having any sons,
the heir to Thrushcross Grange. Through the boy, Heathcliff hopes
to get possession of both houses. The sad, sickly youth is crucial to
Heathcliff for this reason alone: 'he's *mine*, and I want the triumph of
seeing *my* descendant fairly lord of their estates; my child hiring their
children, to till their father's land for wages'. But the boy's weakness
underlines what will eventually be seen as the impotence of Heathcliff's
revenge.

Chapter 7, *pp. 209–25*

Nearly three years pass. Cathy forgets Linton. Nelly Dean hears reports
of his continuing weakness and peevishness.

On her sixteenth birthday, Nelly accompanies Cathy on a ramble
on the moors. Cathy wanders nearer to Wuthering Heights than Nelly
wishes and encounters Heathcliff. He invites the women to the house
and informs Nelly of his plan to marry Linton to Cathy and so secure
Thrushcross Grange (early in the chapter, p. 213). Cathy and Linton
meet and Cathy asks why such near neighbours are not friends. She
receives the briefest of explanations before being sent off with Hareton.

Heathcliff draws attention to the strong contrast between feeble Linton, whom he reckons will not live long after eighteen, and healthy Hareton. Heathcliff rejoices bitterly at his destruction of Hareton. He has ruined a personality of real worth. Linton is nothing beside him yet he shall have everything. The implicit weakness of Heathcliff's revenge is again underlined.

Linton spitefully relishes Hareton's illiteracy.

Cathy tells her father of her expedition the previous day and he forbids her all further dealings with Wuthering Heights. He tells her the story of Heathcliff's treatment of Isabella. Cathy is profoundly affected by it. She has, however, formed an attachment to Linton Heathcliff and begins to write him love letters. Nelly Dean discovers the replies and detects the hand of Heathcliff in them. She takes them and forces from Cathy a confession of her love for Linton, which she laughs at. Knowing the dangers behind the love affair, Nelly burns the letters and requests Linton to write no more.

Chapter 8, *pp. 226-32*

Cathy is saddened by the end of her affair with Linton and wanders on the moors. Her sadness is increased by her intuition of her father's death.

Cathy encounters Heathcliff who informs her that Linton is seriously ill because of the ending of his affair with her. He tells her it is her duty to save him from death and that he will be away from home all that week. Despite Nelly's warnings, Cathy is moved by Heathcliff's story and she eventually persuades Nelly to accompany her to Wuthering Heights to discover the truth.

Chapter 9, *pp. 233-41*

The following morning Cathy and Nelly Dean go to Wuthering Heights where they meet the petulant Linton. Despite his behaviour, Cathy is affectionate towards him. They quarrel about their respective parents' love affair. Nelly describes Linton as 'the worst-tempered bit of a sickly slip that ever struggled into his teens'. However, the young people's love has clearly been revived. If it is only a pale imitation of their parents' love, we can see in it all the uneasy alliance of care and hatred which characterized theirs.

Nelly Dean is laid up in her bed for three weeks after the visit.

Chapter 10, *pp. 242–52*

During Nelly's illness Cathy rides over to see Linton almost every day. Her passion for the boy is strange but clearly strong. The affair is anything but happy. In a description of their different ideas of heaven (p. 245), a contrast is shown between Linton's passivity and Cathy's liveliness.

But Hareton Earnshaw has also fallen in love with Cathy. In a moving attempt to show this he is trying to learn to read. The prospect of love has the effect of redeeming him from his brutishness. Cathy cruelly disregards his efforts. Hareton is deeply jealous of Linton. He threatens him and pursues Cathy who beats him with her whip.

Linton continues to sulk. Cathy threatens to leave him and receives a pathetic account of him and his love (pp. 250–51). Cathy truly loves him despite her recognition of his sadly twisted nature. This is an ironic contrast to the relationship between their parents.

Nelly Dean tells Cathy's father of his daughter's visits to Wuthering Heights and he again orders her to stop going.

Chapter 11, *pp. 253–6*

We are now within a year of Lockwood's arrival on the scene. Nelly Dean mentions the possibility of an attachment between him and Cathy.

Continuing her story, Nelly recounts Edgar's approaching death and his concern for Cathy's future happiness. Hoping that she will secure her rightful inheritance, he agrees to her occasionally seeing

Linton Heathcliff. But Linton is also dying. In retrospect, Nelly Dean
is horrified at the way Heathcliff treats his son.

Chapter 12, *pp. 257–61*

Cathy and Linton meet, but the boy has clearly been forced into the
meeting by his father. Nelly Dean recognizes how seriously ill he is.

Chapter 13, *pp. 262–74*

Both Edgar and Linton are close to death. Cathy is torn between her
responsibilities for both of them.

She visits Linton again. It is obvious that the boy has been terrorized
by his father. He dare not confess how much he is his father's puppet
(p. 264). Heathcliff himself now interrupts them. He bullies Linton
and asks Cathy to walk back with him to Wuthering Heights. She
consents when Linton pleads with her.

Once at Wuthering Heights Heathcliff locks the door: Cathy, Linton
and Nelly Dean are his prisoners. Heathcliff himself now brutally
forces the issue of marriage. Linton confesses that his father wishes
the service to take place the following morning.

Heathcliff returns, having let the women's horses roam away. Cathy
pleads to be set free and she even promises to marry Linton if Heathcliff
will let her return to her dying father. He refuses and takes pleasure
in the suffering he is inflicting. Cathy's passionate appeals to his better
nature are wholly in vain.

A rescue party from the Grange is foiled.

The following morning Cathy is separated from Nelly who is made
a solitary prisoner.

Chapter 14, *pp. 275–82*

On the fifth afternoon of her imprisonment Nelly Dean is freed. She learns that Edgar is close to death.

Linton has now married Cathy. His spiteful nature is clearer than ever (pp. 276–8). He tells Nelly of Heathcliff's brutal treatment of Cathy. Nelly Dean informs Edgar of what has happened. He now realizes that Heathcliff's plan is to secure all his property and he tries to change his will. Heathcliff delays the lawyer and hires him for himself.

Cathy successfully escapes from Wuthering Heights and her father dies quietly in her arms.

Chapter 15, *pp. 283–8*

Heathcliff comes to Thrushcross Grange. He returns to the room where he last saw Catherine eighteen years before. He demands that Cathy return. In an important speech she turns to him and exposes his loveless, wretched state (p. 285). She then agrees to go.

Left alone with Nelly, Heathcliff gives a picture of his macabre passion. In his agony after Catherine's death he has been haunted by her ghost. He felt her presence immediately after her burial but during the next eighteen years it has never quite been visible to him. For Heathcliff these eighteen years with a half-glimpsed ghost have been torture. We have seen their effect on him at the start of the novel (pp. 28–9). He now tells Nelly that he asked the sexton to uncover Catherine's coffin. He has gazed upon her face and has been a little eased. He has also bribed the sexton to pull away one side of Catherine's coffin and extracted from the man his promise to do the same to his when he dies. Thus he and Catherine will be together in death as they never were in life.

Chapter 16, *pp. 289–95*

Nelly Dean is forbidden access to Wuthering Heights but is told by the housekeeper Zillah of Cathy's wretchedness and of Linton Heathcliff's death. Cathy is ill for a fortnight after her husband's death. It transpires that he has left all his property to his father. Heathcliff claims Thrushcross Grange 'in his wife's right, and his also'. Cathy, like Hareton, is now penniless.

Zillah tells Nelly Dean of the relationship between Cathy and Hareton. On Cathy's part it is one of almost total hostility. Her presence, however, has an effect on Hareton who wishes to alter his boorish behaviour. Cathy rebuffs him cruelly.

Lockwood, his strength restored, decides to return to London.

Chapter 17, *pp. 296–301*

Lockwood goes to Wuthering Heights to tell Heathcliff he is leaving. Heathcliff is out but Lockwood sees Cathy again. She is dreary and bitter.

Lockwood gives her a letter from Nelly Dean. Cathy is moved at receiving it but cannot reply.

It transpires that Hareton has stolen her books in his continuing effort to learn to read. Cathy is clearly contemptuous of this and Hareton angrily throws the books on to the fire.

Before departing, Lockwood shares a joyless meal with Hareton and Heathcliff.

Chapter 18, *pp. 302–13*

Lockwood returns the following autumn. He discovers that Nelly Dean has moved to Wuthering Heights from Thrushcross Grange. He goes to Wuthering Heights and finds the place much softened and improved. He witnesses a touching scene between Cathy and Hareton. Nelly

Dean informs him that Heathcliff has died three months previously.

Within a fortnight of Lockwood leaving, Nelly Dean was summoned to Wuthering Heights by Heathcliff. This marked a change in his behaviour for prior to this she had been forbidden to come to the house.

The growing relationship between Cathy and Hareton is delicately shown. Hareton is being tamed and civilized through love. This positive and happy note is of the greatest importance, contrasting strongly with Heathcliff's bitter vengefulness.

Chapter 19, *pp. 314–22*

This chapter shows the growing bond of love between Cathy and Hareton and the decline of the loveless Heathcliff.

Cathy and Hareton clear some of Joseph's prized bushes to make a garden. Joseph threatens to leave. Heathcliff is furious that they have dared to touch his property, but Cathy, armed with the assurance of Hareton's love and strength, defies him. Looking into her eyes, Heathcliff relents. We have already seen how much she reminds him of his own Catherine.

Hareton retains a primitive loyalty to Heathcliff but Nelly Dean is sure (pp. 318–19) that he can be made into a decent human being.

Confronted by both Cathy and Hareton, Heathcliff is rendered powerless. They both remind him too excruciatingly of Catherine and all he has lost. He says to Nelly Dean, 'the entire world is a dreadful collection of memoranda that she did exist, and that I have lost her!' The power of Heathcliff's hatred – once an elemental force – is rapidly diminishing. In a most important speech to Nelly Dean (near the end of the chapter, pp. 319–21) he describes his decline. He has, he says 'lost the faculty of enjoying their destruction, and I am too idle to destroy for nothing'.

Confronted by the love of Cathy and Hareton and their reminder of his love for Catherine, Heathcliff's evil fades and with it Heathcliff himself; he longs for death. Nelly Dean believes that 'conscience had turned his heart into an earthly hell'.

Chapter 20, *pp. 323–34*

The dying Heathcliff is in a state of elation. He becomes more solitary and does not eat. The presence of Catherine is closer to him than ever before. He has his vision of his Heaven and longs to die. But the vision is relentless and painful. Even Heathcliff can barely stand it.

While he is dying, Nelly Dean wonders if he is indeed a man or some evil spirit. She ponders the unsolved mystery of his birth.

At his death Heathcliff is wholly unrepentant and only Hareton, whom he has most wronged, mourns for him. Heathcliff is buried next to Catherine. Only Nelly Dean and Hareton accompany his coffin. The country people say that Heathcliff's ghost haunts the neighbourhood.

Hareton and Cathy are to be married and live at Thrushcross Grange.

Before leaving, Lockwood visits the graveyard and ponders the fates of those lying there.

Characters

Heathcliff

Heathcliff bestrides the novel and no simple account can do justice to the richness, depth and variety of his personality. He is as powerful and amoral as the forces of nature with which he is often compared. He is both worldly and profoundly romantic. Love and hatred merge in him and both are extreme.

His origins are unknown. This gives him not only the pathos of the orphan but an air of mystery that deepens into the suspicion that he is connected with the devil. From the start he brings destruction; but the passionate, self-willed little boy can also inspire love. He and Catherine wander freely on the moors. They are natural extroverts. The grandeur of their surroundings enters their souls and their love is like a natural force. As Nelly Dean declares: 'it was one of their chief amusements to run away to the moors in the morning and remain there all day, and the after punishment grew a mere thing to laugh at.'

And punished they certainly are, particularly Heathcliff. If he can attract the love of Catherine and her father, he also gains the enmity of her brother, Hindley. Hindley gets revenge by reducing Heathcliff to the status of a servant. For some time Heathcliff is not unduly upset by this. He is a child of nature. The distinctions he recognizes are those of drive, personality and passion rather than class. The dreary, religious dogmatism of Joseph has no effect on him either beyond stirring his impulse to revolt.

These features of Heathcliff's youthful personality are particularly clear in the scene where he and Catherine look in at the Lintons' window.

He and Catherine have been wandering together on the moors in defiance of Joseph's dreary Sunday regime. Both children are tough and natural. They steal through the garden and cling to the window ledge to look in (p. 48). Heathcliff responds to the luxurious room directly and sensuously. He and Catherine, however, share one reaction to the children they see: contempt. 'We laughed outright at the petted things, we did despise them! When would you catch me wishing to have what Catherine wanted? or find us by ourselves, seeking entertainment in yelling, and sobbing, and rolling on the ground, divided by the whole room?' But these natural children are far from 'nice'. They make noises deliberately to terrify the Lintons. The dogs are set on them and if Heathcliff can relish Catherine's beautiful hair and recognize that 'she is so immeasurably superior to them', he also admires her tomboy courage when she is caught by the dog. However, the incident marks the end of childish naïvety. The Lintons treat Catherine as a lady and Heathcliff as a servant. They will never again share completely and easily each other's thoughts and lives.

Catherine is taught to be a lady. A veneer of civilization covers her natural self. This acquired rather than natural behaviour hurts Heathcliff deeply. He tries to match up to it, but as Nelly Dean grooms him we see the wild and diabolic elements in Heathcliff that mark his body as well as his soul:

Do you mark those two lines between your eyes, and those thick brows that instead of rising arched, sink in the middle, and that couple of black fiends, so deeply buried, who never open their windows boldly, but lurk glinting under them, like devil's spies (middle of chapter, p. 56)?

Almost immediately Heathcliff lashes out at Edgar and, after punishment from Hindley, vows his revenge. Frustrated love and vengeance, the keynotes throughout Heathcliff's adult life, are sounded. The ineradicable traces of the devil will assert themselves.

One great betrayal is required before this comes about: Catherine's refusal to marry Heathcliff because he is socially inferior (pp. 76–83). Heathcliff's presence – his power, virility, that in him which is so much stronger than the veneer of culture – has entered Catherine's soul. She is bound utterly to him, to him and the moors of which he is a part. There is nothing heavenly in the Heathcliff she loves. He is the earth and perhaps the devils under it. So absolute is his effect on her that she can truthfully say 'he's more myself than I am'.

This is what she betrays, and the passions in Heathcliff which run so much deeper than mere morals are perverted to destruction. Heathcliff goes away that night and acquires (in this novel of the emotions it is unnecessary to know how) the money and bearing he requires for his revenge.

Heathcliff returns a seeming gentleman but his new appearance cannot hide the blackness and ferocity of his true temperament. The pleasantness of Catherine's and Edgar's marriage evaporates in the presence of this 'fierce, pitiless, wolfish man'. For both Heathcliff and Catherine, love and hatred merge into an obsession, the only end of which can be death.

Their last earthly meeting is described in Chapter 1, Volume II. However, before this takes place, Emily Brontë is careful to present the evil and destructive side of Heathcliff. We see him getting the hopelessly alcoholic Hindley into his power and, far worse, his corruption of Hareton into little more than an animal. He is also preparing emotional torture for Isabella. The Heathcliff who holds the fading Catherine in his arms is profoundly evil for all that he inspires our compassion. We cannot measure Heathcliff by conventional standards. He is too awe-inspiring and too ambiguous.

Nonetheless, it is Catherine's choice in marriage of the conventional Edgar which destroys both her and Heathcliff. Heathcliff knows that she is dying as soon as he sees her, but he knows also that she committed emotional suicide long before. The thought of her death drives him almost to distraction. For a moment we forget his evil in the pathos of his account of his ruined life, his cheated passion and his desolate future:

You teach me how cruel you've been – cruel and false. *Why* did you despise me? *Why* did you betray your own heart, Cathy? I have not one word of comfort – you deserve this. You have killed yourself. Yes, you may kiss me and cry; and wring out my kisses and tears. They'll blight you – they'll damn you. You loved me – then what *right* had you to leave me? What right – answer me – for the poor fancy you felt for Linton? Because misery, and degradation, and death, and nothing that God or satan could inflict would have parted us, *you* of your own will, did it. I have not broken your heart – *you* have broken it – and in breaking it, you have broken mine. So much the worse for me, that I am strong. Do I want to live? What kind of living will it be when you – oh, God! would *you* like to live with your soul in the grave (near end of chapter, pp. 160–61)?

We glimpse that for Heathcliff there is one absolute morality: the joy of unrestrained passion fulfilled. Cheated of this, conventional decency, Edgar's decency, is woefully inadequate. After Catherine's death the primitive, evil and profoundly romantic aspects of Heathcliff's personality rise to the surface. When Nelly Dean tells him that Catherine has died: 'He dashed his head against the knotted trunk; and, lifting up his eyes, howled, not like a man, but like a savage beast getting goaded to death with knives and spears.' He begs that he may be haunted by Catherine and in his frenzied state goes to her grave and begins to dig up her coffin (pp. 286–7). He desperately needs some sign of her continuing presence. While he is digging he believes that he feels Catherine's ghost very close to him. She will haunt him for the rest of his life. It is this agonized, haunted Heathcliff that we are first introduced to. His whole being throbs with remembered passion and pain from the tantalizing elusiveness of the ghost (pp. 28, 29 and 286–7).

But while Heathcliff is capable of this bizarre and extreme behaviour he is also fulfilling his vow of worldly revenge. He works the destruction of Isabella, Hindley and Hareton and becomes the monster of Wuthering Heights. He derives great pleasure from this. The man of passion can also completely disregard the feelings of others. This is particularly clear in the treatment of his son: Heathcliff despises Linton utterly but he needs him for his plans. He needs him to secure possession of Thrushcross Grange and he needs him as his heir. He tries to manipulate the affair between Linton and Cathy, going so far as to make Cathy a prisoner and forcing the marriage.

But Emily Brontë's interests go far deeper than the creation of mere sensation and the thrill of revenge. She is concerned to show that not

only is evil destructive but that it is self-destructive. The full measure
of Heathcliff's revenge is thwarted by the love between those whom
he wishes to destroy and by the memory of the depth of his own love
(p. 319). Heathcliff has tried to destroy Hareton and to humiliate Cathy.
He is able to reduce them to the level of an animal and a servant. What
he cannot do is destroy their ability to love each other. Neither can he
obliterate the strong resemblance that each bears to Catherine. For
Heathcliff 'the entire world is a dreadful collection of memoranda that
she did exist, and that I have lost her'. Throughout *Wuthering Heights*
we have seen people fade and corrupt in the face of Heathcliff's animal
vitality. We now see him – and his evil – wither in the face of love and
remembered passion.

The dying Heathcliff becomes increasingly remote from the world
he has mastered and tried to destroy. The cruelly insistent ghost of
Catherine saps his potency:

'It is a poor conclusion, is it not,' he observed, having brooded a while on
the scene he had just witnessed. 'An absurd termination to my violent exertions?
I get levers and mattocks to demolish the two houses, and train myself to be
capable of working like Hercules, and when everything is ready, and in my
power, I find the will to lift a slate off either roof has vanished! My old enemies
have not beaten me – now would be the precise time to revenge myself on
their representatives – I could do it; and none could hinder me – But where
is the use? I don't care for striking, I can't take the trouble to raise my hand!
That sounds as if I had been labouring the whole time, only to exhibit a fine
trace of magnanimity. It is far from being the case – I have lost the faculty of
enjoying their destruction, and I am too idle to destroy for nothing' (end of
chapter, pp. 319–20).

Heathcliff is unrepentant to the end. He lives increasingly in the
world of Catherine's ghost and with the longing that his body should
lie beside hers and rot. He remains an awesome figure. Even Nelly
Dean remains undecided if he was wholly a man or 'a ghoul, or a
vampire'. In the end, his attempt to destroy the Earnshaws and the
Lintons results in their happy union, in the married love of Cathy and
Hareton.

Catherine Earnshaw

Catherine's whole being is bound to Heathcliff's. This is clear even from her childhood diary. She is a very lively, very attractive little girl:

Her spirits were always at high-water mark, her tongue always going — singing, laughing, and plaguing everybody who would not do the same. A wild wick slip she was – but she had the bonniest eyes, and the sweetest smile, and lightest foot in the parish; and, after all, I believe she meant no harm; for once she made you cry in good earnest, it seldom happened that she would not keep you company and oblige you to be quiet that you might comfort her (beginning of chapter, p. 42).

Like Heathcliff, she is a child of nature: spontaneous, passionate, tough. She is his ideal companion. She shares his wild life until the Lintons assert their hold upon her and she is made into a lady (p. 52). In the five weeks she stays with the Lintons her natural feelings and ambitions are covered with the veneer of respectability. This is fatal for her. She can no longer look on Heathcliff with the direct simplicity of her childhood. This is clear as soon as she returns to Wuthering Heights. She asks for Heathcliff almost at once and when she finds him she smothers him with kisses. Then she draws back. She laughs at him. Later, when Heathcliff has been beaten, she runs to comfort him and suffers for his unhappiness, but the divide between her impulsiveness and her acquired respectability is clear (Chapter 7). It is made more obvious as her affair with Edgar Linton develops.

Nelly Dean declares that Catherine has now taken on a 'double character'. There is the Catherine that Heathcliff loves and the young lady that Edgar is courting (Chapter 8). For all that this double character is not openly dishonest or hypocritical, it causes Catherine great strain. In Chapter 8 we see her reprove Heathcliff for being boorish but we also see that the proper young lady she becomes for Edgar's sake cannot restrain her passionate temperament. Edgar is appalled by her behaviour, but such is Catherine's magnetism that he cannot leave her (p. 72).

Nor can Catherine leave him. She has affection for Edgar and when she agrees to marry him it is not simply to enhance her social status. But she refuses Heathcliff because she believes that marriage with him would degrade her. In the scene of her confession to Nelly Dean, her anguish at her decision and the true nature of her passion are vividly shown (pp. 76–83). Catherine is bound body and soul to Heathcliff, to the moors and to earthly passion. Her speech reaches the heights of poetry as she describes the universe that is contained in Heathcliff. She then declares:

My love for Heathcliff resembles the eternal rocks beneath – a source of little visible delight, but necessary. Nelly, I *am* Heathcliff – he's always, always in my mind – not as a pleasure, any more than I am always a pleasure to myself – but, as my own being . . . (middle of chapter, p. 82).

There is nothing sweet or sentimental about this. Catherine knows perfectly well how dark and how sinister Heathcliff is. She is a full-blooded and natural person. She recognizes that love has its darkness and brutality and she accepts these unquestioningly. In this scene she lays bare her soul and then admits she has offered her love to the wrong man. She does not marry Edgar simply for his money but she refuses Heathcliff because he has not got any. By making this great refusal she kills her soul and, eventually, herself. Heathcliff forces her to recognize this when he rounds on her in Chapter 1, Volume II (pp. 160–61).

Catherine's marriage to Edgar is described by Nelly Dean (pp. 91–2). It is not a wholly easy relationship. Both Edgar and his sister stand in some awe of Catherine and are frightened by her volatile temper. However, 'she seemed almost over fond of Mr Linton: and even to his sister, she showed plenty of affection'. Nelly Dean compares Catherine to a thorny rose and the Lintons to honeysuckle.

With the return of Heathcliff the marriage is destroyed. Catherine is thrown into the wildest excitement by his presence and her girlish high spirits are now seen as the emotional instability of the mature woman. She recognizes clearly Heathcliff's 'fierce, pitiless, wolfish' nature but her attraction to him is irresistible and she is contemptuous of Edgar's mildness and decency (p. 116).

What Catherine suffers now are the effects of her refusal to free herself to the flood of her emotions. The love and the passion inside her can find no easy outlet. Instead, they turn in upon themselves, and bring her to the point of breakdown. She is feverish and her thwarted passion is killing her. She cries out:

> Oh, I'm burning! I wish I were out of doors – I wish I were a girl again, half savage and hardy, and free . . . and laughing at injuries, not maddening under them! Why am I so changed? Why does my blood rush into a hell of tumult at a few words? I'm sure I should be myself were I once again among the heather on those hills . . . (middle of chapter, p. 124).

Her mind is set on death and her appearance has altered so that 'there seemed unearthly beauty in the change'. But if Catherine has changed, she has not softened. There is a 'wild vindictiveness' in her face and also in her words. Her accusations of Heathcliff's future infidelity and forgetfulness of her torture him, and as she looks despairingly round the world she is leaving, she realizes that her sufferings will continue beyond the grave (p. 159). The spontaneous, passionate tomboy of a little girl has become a fearsome and unworldly wraith. Even death is no deliverance for her and she seems to live on in a half life as a ghost torturing Heathcliff to near madness and death.

Though Catherine makes a fatal compromise with her emotions, they reassert themselves and destroy her. In so doing they raise her to an awe-inspiring level. Eventually her passion does match Heathcliff's but they can meet only in death, in the slow corruption of their bodies in their adjoining coffins.

Edgar Linton

It is largely through Nelly Dean that our opinion of Edgar forms and changes. He never achieves the romantic stature of Catherine and Heathcliff. Emily Brontë did not mean him to. But what Nelly does come to admire in him is his Christian fortitude after Catherine's death:

Time brought resignation, and a melancholy sweeter than common joy. He recalled her memory with ardent, tender love, and hopeful aspiring to the better world, where he doubted not, she was gone (end of chapter, p. 182).

This reaction is in marked contrast to Hindley's alcoholic decline on the death of his wife and also, of course, to Heathcliff's behaviour.

Heathcliff, naturally, wholly despises Edgar and in despising him rejects the simple human decency that Edgar represents. He describes him as 'that insipid, paltry creature attending Catherine from *duty* and *humanity*! From *pity* and *charity*!' The sad fact is that these wholly worthy virtues are utterly inappropriate to the real Catherine. She lives, as Heathcliff well knows, beyond the bounds of such conventional morality.

Heathcliff and Catherine have the effect of making the good seem inadequate. However, we should beware of labelling Edgar simply as virtuous. If he does stand for good, conventional things, he is also peevish and weak, particularly as a boy. But he is a complex character and we can neither wholly like him nor wholly dismiss him.

We share Heathcliff's contempt for him when we are shown him as the petulant little boy in the Lintons' drawing-room (p. 48). This feeling is intensified when he unintentionally taunts Heathcliff at Wuthering Heights (p. 58). Later, when Edgar is courting Catherine, Nelly Dean draws an important contrast between the two:

The contrast resembled what you see in exchanging a bleak, hilly, coal country for a beautiful fertile valley; and his voice and greeting were as opposite as his aspect – He had a sweet, low manner of speaking, and pronounced his words as you do, that's less gruff than we talk here and softer (end of chapter, p. 69).

Edgar is a civilized, pleasant young man but weak and easily shocked. He is rightly horrified at Catherine's treatment of Nelly Dean and he tries to leave Wuthering Heights. His resolution fails him and the 'soft thing', as Nelly calls him, returns to his fate (p. 71–2). Edgar declares his love for a woman whose fundamentally passionate nature he can neither understand nor match. We begin to pity him.

From the start of the marriage he is slightly afraid of Catherine's volatile temper, but it should be noted that the marriage *is* a relatively successful one (pp. 91–2). Under normal circumstances Edgar is a good husband. But he cannot compete with the forces of nature, with Heathcliff or the passion roused in Catherine. From now until his death he is one of Heathcliff's victims. He knows perfectly well how evil Heathcliff is and he tells him so:

'I have been so far forbearing with you, sir,' he said, quietly; 'not that I was ignorant of your miserable, degraded character, but, I felt that you were only partly responsible for that; and Catherine, wishing to keep up your acquaintance, I acquiesced – foolishly. Your presence is a moral poison that would contaminate the most virtuous – for that cause, and to prevent worse consequences, I shall deny you, hereafter, admission into the house, and give notice, now, that I require your instant departure' (middle of chapter, p. 113).

Poor Edgar is quite right in what he says and threatens to do. Nonetheless, he appears cowardly, weak and ultimately somewhat contemptible. He can sulk, plot and try to defend his wife and his sister but he has no chance against Heathcliff whatsoever. He must suffer because Catherine chose *him* rather than her true love. Edgar will be obliged to nurse his wife while she dies for love of another man. He will have to disown his sister, and when he is prepared to take in her child he will have it snatched away by Heathcliff. Much later, when Edgar is dying, Heathcliff will also abduct his daughter and force her marriage so as to secure Thrushcross Grange, Edgar's house. Even when Edgar tries to prevent all this happening we discover that Heathcliff has hired the local lawyer before him and has defeated him (pp. 279–81). His one consolation is the love of his daughter and he dies in her arms.

A weak man pitted against impossible odds, Edgar tries to uphold conventional moral values but is destroyed by forces beyond his control.

Isabella Linton

Like her brother, Isabella is somewhat weak and, at times, peevish. However, she does not have an unattractive personality, and she is called upon to show much spirit.

Her chief function in the novel is to be a tragic puppet. She falls hopelessly and blindly in love with Heathcliff, wholly unaware of his callous designs on her (pp. 100–106 and 148–9). Heathcliff degrades her atrociously and she shows her finest spirit when she runs away and destroys her wedding ring. She goes to London where, eventually, she dies, leaving behind her son, the vicious and sickly Linton Heathcliff.

Hers is a tragic life. She can love passionately; she can hate in equal measure. She is perfectly capable of running away with the man she loves and of taunting him cruelly when she realizes his true nature. However, like her brother, she is pitted against forces for which she is no match.

Hindley Earnshaw

Hindley is a profoundly neurotic character. As such he plays an important part in setting the tone of the novel. He is Heathcliff's first great enemy. As a child, Hindley is intensely jealous of the affection Heathcliff inspires in old Mr Earnshaw and gets revenge by degrading Heathcliff to the level of a servant and humiliating him in front of Catherine. As a boy, Heathcliff is determined on revenge and the scene prepares us for the mature Heathcliff of the second part of the novel.

When Heathcliff returns a rich man he stays with Hindley at Wuthering Heights. Hindley's wife has died by this time and Hindley himself has sunk into depravity and alcoholism. He has left his son to his own devices and Hareton too has sunk to a level little better than an animal. Heathcliff exploits both these situations. He gambles with Hindley and wins from him the whole of his worldly wealth: Wuthering Heights. He further depraves Hareton as part of his plan to ruin the Earnshaws forever. Spurred to some sort of action, Hindley tries to murder Heathcliff but fails and, in his turn, dies.

In Hindley are concentrated the themes of spitefulness, personal weakness and the ease with which men can sink into depravity. His tragic and sordid life is an essential element in the atmosphere of the novel.

Cathy Linton

Cathy has an important part to play in the novel and Emily Brontë skilfully creates her character. She had to picture someone who was a recognizable daughter of Catherine Earnshaw but not a rival. She had, in addition, to make her both a victim of Heathcliff and a character stronger in a different way.

As a child she is delightful. Nelly Dean gives an important description of her:

> She was the most winning thing that ever brought sunshine into a desolate house – a real beauty in face – with the Earnshaws' handsome dark eyes, but the Lintons' fair skin, and small features, and yellow curling hair. Her spirit was high though not rough, and qualified by a heart, sensitive and lively to excess in its affections. That capacity for intense attachments reminded me of her mother; still she did not resemble her; for she could be soft and mild as a dove, and she had a gentle voice, and pensive expression: her anger was never furious, her love never fierce; it was deep and tender (beginning of chapter, p. 187).

This is in marked contrast to the Cathy we meet at the start of the novel who is bitter and shrewish. It is a measure of Heathcliff's destructive power that he can so pervert such a good nature, though it should be remembered that Nelly Dean qualifies her early praise by noting 'a propensity to be saucy' as one of Cathy's failings. Nonetheless, it is clear that the fundamental parts of Cathy's personality are strong, positive and good. It is through them that redemption comes.

Despite his obnoxious and peevish weakness she genuinely loves

Linton Heathcliff. They squabble, for Cathy is no more sweet or sentimental than her mother. Her love, however, is of a different quality: it is more genuinely caring. She is not attracted to Heathcliff in the slightest: she finds him repellent and is not afraid to say so (p. 285). Cathy knows what love is and she can inspire it in both Linton and Hareton. She is also plucky and high spirited. With these qualities she can animate even Linton and she is prepared to put herself at some risk for his sake. Eventually she is made Heathcliff's prisoner and forced to marry Linton. She escapes briefly to be with her dying father but is summoned back by Heathcliff. Cathy is left penniless when Linton dies and so begins that wretched part of her life in which we see her at the start of the novel.

Cathy is obliged to spend much of her time with Hareton. If Cathy is a delightful, brave and high-spirited girl, her treatment of Hareton is poor from the first time she sees him (p. 216). She is repelled by his brutishness and is reluctant to believe that he is her cousin. She joins Linton in baiting him and reveals a distinctly cruel streak. Hareton, however, has fallen deeply in love with her. Heathcliff has done his best to destroy Hareton. The boy is an illiterate boor. However, the hope of love is not so easily destroyed and Hareton makes efforts to improve himself and be more acceptable to Cathy. Cathy cruelly and repeatedly snubs these efforts. As her lonely imprisonment at Wuthering Heights continues she becomes increasingly hostile to him as to everything. When Lockwood comes to give notice he tries to encourage Cathy to help Hareton (pp. 298–9). The result is that she is crueller to him than ever. This shows very clearly the continuing evil effects of Heathcliff's revenge. He seems able to destroy even the younger generation. The beautiful and passionate little girl has been turned into a shrew. Any love, and with it the hope of improvement that her beauty inspires in Hareton, is likewise dashed.

But as Heathcliff fades so does his ability to do evil. Cathy's conscience begins to prick her (p. 308). Slowly but with great persistence she begins to win Hareton over. By the time of the incident with Joseph's garden (pp. 314–16) Hareton and Cathy can present something of a united front against Heathcliff. He realizes this but such is his decline that he has not the will to destroy them. That he still could he knows perfectly well, but he is reminded too much of his own affair with Catherine. Their love and his remembered passion make him increasingly powerless. Hopes of vengeance fade, and with the death of Heathcliff the life-giving power of Cathy's love grows in strength until Hareton is the redeemed man Lockwood sees on his return visit (pp. 304–5). She and Hareton, we learn, are to be married.

Cathy is an attractive and complex character. She is plucky, passionate and essentially good. Though like her mother in some ways, the quality of her love is very different. It has nothing of the grandly obsessive and its natural conclusion is not death but marriage. Cathy's is the love that brings life and fruition. Again, she is neither soft nor sentimental. She has a temper and a streak of cruelty. Far more important, however, she has very great strength and perseverance. It is through her that something of the evil in the novel is redeemed and evil itself shown to be finally self-destructive.

Hareton Earnshaw

Left to his own devices by his drunken father, Hareton is almost wrecked by Heathcliff. He is an interesting and important character. A number of major themes in the novel centre on him.

In his degradation and boorishness he shows Emily Brontë's concern with the thin veneer of civilization. People revert to an animal level very easily in *Wuthering Heights*. Hindley Earnshaw, Heathcliff when Catherine shows increasing interest in Edgar (p. 67), and Hareton himself all reveal this weakness. Heathcliff takes pleasure in the corruption of Hareton. His revenge is particularly telling because he knows that he is working on a potentially fine spirit. Hareton is a much finer man than Heathcliff's own son and Heathcliff takes a bitter pleasure in this:

'I've pleasure in him!' he continued reflecting aloud. 'He has satisfied my expectations – if he were born a fool I should not enjoy it half so much – But he's no fool; and I can sympathise with all his feelings, having felt them myself – I know what he suffers now, for instance, exactly – it is merely a beginning of what he shall suffer, though. And he'll never be able to emerge from his bathos of coarseness, and ignorance. I've got him faster than his scoundrel of a father secured me, and lower; for he takes a pride in his brutishness. I've taught him to scorn everything extra-animal as silly and weak – Don't you think Hindley would be proud of his son, if he could see him? almost as proud as I am of mine – But there's this difference, one is gold put to the use of paving stones; and the other is tin polished to ape a service of silver – *Mine* has nothing valuable about it; yet I shall have the merit of making it go as far as such poor stuff can go. *His* had first-rate qualities, and they are lost – rendered worse than unavailing – I have nothing to regret; he would have more than any, but I, are aware of – And the best of it is, Hareton is damnably fond of me . . . (middle of chapter, p. 217).

The profitless viciousness of Heathcliff's revenge is obvious here and what he says is largely true. The Hareton of most of the novel is vicious and bad tempered. He throws stones at visitors, hangs animals and cannot read. We are made aware too, however, that he is not a fool and that there could be some hope for him. He can respond to the beauty of a woman and he is keen to improve himself. His constant rebuffs make him show his soured nature, but we also see his persistence. He steals Cathy's books in his struggle to improve himself and when he burns them (p. 299) in a fit of pique, it is not without some regret.

Heathcliff is also right when he says that Hareton loves him. He has an unquestioning feudal loyalty to his destroyer. Even when his love affair with Cathy is some way advanced he will not allow her to speak ill of him (p. 318). He is also the only true mourner at Heathcliff's funeral and Emily Brontë provides a most touching picture of grief (p. 332).

But Heathcliff is wrong when he claims the damage he has inflicted is irreparable. Nelly Dean believes Hareton can be helped and it is her natural and practical kindness that finally persuades Cathy that she should help him. The process is not an altogether simple one and perhaps Nelly Dean exaggerates when she uses the word 'rapidly'. Nonetheless, the substance of her account (pp. 318–19) is correct. It is this redeeming power of love that has changed Hareton into the respectable, handsome young man Lockwood sees on his return (p. 304).

It is largely through the figure of Hareton Earnshaw that Emily

Brontë conveys the idea that evil does not finally triumph and that love is a stronger force.

Linton Heathcliff

Linton Heathcliff is a pathetic, unpleasant character. Nelly Dean describes him with uncharacteristic harshness as 'the worst tempered bit of a sickly slip that ever struggled into its teens! Happily, as Mr Heathcliff conjectured, he'll not win twenty!'

Linton's extreme frailty is clear from the moment we first see him (p. 198) and when Heathcliff comes to claim him, his contempt for him is obvious. Linton is no more to Heathcliff than 'property' and his sole interest in him is to secure Thrushcross Grange through his marriage to Cathy and so complete his revenge. He terrorizes the boy utterly and reduces him to a mere puppet (Chapter 12, Volume II).

While Linton can inspire great affection in Cathy, it is difficult to see that this is really returned. Linton is a spiteful and selfish invalid, constantly seeking attention but offering little interest in return. He also lacks the strength to conduct his love affair with much conviction. The inspiration behind it is far more his father's desire than his own. He is only really interested in himself. He constantly tries to gain attention and is petulant, peevish and argumentative. He frequently upsets Cathy despite her obvious affection and the considerable risks she runs in showing it. The fundamental difference between them is shown in the descriptions of their respective ideas of heaven. Cathy's is lively and healthy, Linton's is passive (p. 245).

When Linton dies he leaves everything to his father. Cathy is penniless.

Nelly Dean

Nelly Dean is the principal narrator of the story. As such she is concerned in nearly every episode. Throughout she commands our warmth and respect. She is a brave, forthright and good-natured woman and a perfect foil to all of the characters. She is well read and Lockwood recognizes that she has thought deeply about things (p. 62). She is a practical woman and a good nurse. We feel that her joy over the final marriage of Cathy and Hareton enhances its value.

Involved in the whole narrative, Nelly Dean is, by necessity, the confidante of most of the major characters. They nearly all respect her and look to her for kindness, common sense or a sympathetic ear. But Nelly is far from being a passive woman. When Heathcliff comes to her telling her that he wants to reform and 'be good' her advice is quite sharp. When Catherine tells her of her decision to marry Edgar she is even more forthright. It is a measure of the respect in which she is held that not only can she talk to the young mistress in the way she does but that she is listened to.

Throughout the extreme and often bizarre events that take place or are reported in the novel, Nelly Dean goes on her way sympathetic, helpful and level-headed. Even as an adult, Heathcliff continues to confide in her, confessing that he has tried to dig up Catherine's grave. This earns a reproof. We see again that he has some respect for her when she asks him to leave the house after his last meeting with Catherine. It is Nelly who brings him the news of her death and she who sees him howl. But if Heathcliff preserves a respect for Nelly he does not allow it to get in the way of his plans. He is quite capable of locking her away while he forces the marriage between Cathy and Linton and it is significant that when he too has finally died Nelly is left speculating on his origins and his possible association with the devil (p. 327).

Nelly is also the confidante of others whom Heathcliff has forced to suffer. It is to her that Isabella writes when she has realized Heathcliff's true nature and, perhaps most important of all, it is she who urges Cathy to lead Hareton back to humanity.

Nelly's beliefs are conventional, kind and strong. The goodness of her heart and the courage of her convictions enable her to appreciate and assess all of the events that take place in the book. We feel that she is an integral part of the final triumph of goodness, decency and love.

Joseph

Joseph has little to do with the plot of *Wuthering Heights* but contributes greatly to its atmosphere. His strongly marked dialect is of vital importance for providing local colour and authenticity.

He also serves as a contrast first to the morality of love that finally emerges and secondly to the grand amorality of the passion of Heathcliff whose servant he becomes. His dour, extreme and hypocritical Christianity casts gloom everywhere. As such, it is a useful means of evoking the negative mood of the opening of the novel. It is more important however as yet another foil to the type of love that triumphs in the end. It is significant that Emily Brontë uses the destruction of Joseph's garden to show the strength that Cathy and Hareton have found in their love. For all his concern with morality, Joseph is a life-denying hypocrite, scarcely above the lowest levels of behaviour shown in the novel.

Lockwood

Mr Lockwood is a rather pale creature, a city fop set among basic, passionate country people. It is significant that the greater part of the novel is related to him while he is ill. He has almost no place among the leading characters, despite Nelly Dean's brief wish that he might marry Cathy and so save her (p. 295). Attracted though he is to the girl, he is not an earnest lover as his brief account of a previous affair shows. When he sees Cathy restored to good spirits through her love for Hareton he regrets his lost chance.

Commentary

Atmosphere

Above all, *Wuthering Heights* is a love story. The passions involved are exceptionally violent and the novel is suffused with a wild and unforgettable poetry. The great scenes: the haunted Heathcliff's sobbing to Catherine's ghost; Catherine's confession of her love; the incomparable last meeting of the two; Heathcliff's hearing of Catherine's death and his subsequent suffering; these are some of the greatest moments in the English novel. They are extreme and they are melodramatic. They appeal to a level far deeper than reason or common sense.

Emily Brontë intended this. She knew that emotion may be violent and, when violent, ruthless. Through nearly all of her characters emotional energy rushes with the turmoil and elemental force of a storm. Such passions can ennoble and deprave. But Emily Brontë is not concerned with passing easy moral judgements. She raises our sense of awe and makes us realize the scope and danger of forces common to all people but rarely experienced to such a degree. Through the passions of her characters she quickens our own and she leaves us with an enhanced sense of life.

To do this required exceptional insight, certainty and skill. She knows all of her characters wholly and so she can contrast them and provide the continuous variety which helps to make up the novel's power and, in part, its meaning. She knew the quiet, strong goodness of Nelly Dean and the depravity of Hindley. She had entered into the girlish liveliness of Catherine as thoroughly as her adult suffering. In her greatest creation, Heathcliff, she shows she understood not only exceptional and virile ardour but how closely that lives with the vicious and the evil. Finally, she knew that such desires are enfeebled in the presence of another sort of love, a love that is caring and creative. She juxtaposes these two forms of love. The way they relate to each other, the way that the positive love of Cathy and Hareton develops from the grand, fatal love of Heathcliff and Catherine, is one of the most important things she has to show us. And it is the showing that is important. Emily Brontë does not ask us to choose, she asks us to see and feel.

But in addition to understanding passionate complexities, Emily Brontë needed a knowledge of her craft. Her novel required extremes and these would be merely silly had she not been able to place them in a real setting. Look at the opening chapters again. Most of what she had to do is concentrated there. Lockwood comes to a forbidding house and is trapped in a snowstorm. He falls asleep and has nightmares. He reads about a mysterious past in an old Bible. He sees his grim, strange gypsy host cry out after a ghost. This could be just corny. It isn't corny because of the very real world in which it takes place; a world of pewter plates and tea-caddies, of fires and dogs and window latches. And then the sheer imaginative conviction of the whole compels our belief. It rings true to our experiences of being half awake in a nightmare.

Strangeness, the wild unfamiliarity of provincial Yorkshire, are also important. These are stressed by Lockwood at the start. Through the detail he gives, Emily Brontë provides much local colour. We see how basic even fairly substantial houses are. We see too how basic are the lives of the people who live in them. Above all we see how close they live to nature.

All of this has the effect of increasing the sense of distance between the ordinary lives of Emily Brontë's characters and the greater number of her readers. It is through her eye for concrete detail, however, that we are kept firmly in a real world despite the bizarre nature of the events described.

And throughout we are aware of the moors, the wildness of the countryside and of the weather. Lockwood is caught in a snowstorm. Catherine becomes feverish after walking in a storm. The older Mr and Mrs Linton die from exposure to the same one. Nature is often harsh and extreme. The people are similar. Even when they are dead the moors invade the part of the churchyard in which they are buried.

While Emily Brontë uses nature and the moors for some of her most extreme effects, we should also notice that with the moors can be associated a far different type of love from that between Catherine and Heathcliff. Primroses grow there and gardens can be salvaged. Summer days are pleasant and as natural and supportive of the type of love that goes with them as winter is wild and destructive.

Throughout, the heavily contrasted atmospheres of *Wuthering Heights* support what Emily Brontë has to describe.

Style

The style also helps. The greater part of the novel is narrated by Nelly Dean to the ailing Lockwood. Slyly, Emily Brontë has him say: 'she is, on the whole, a very fair narrator, I don't think I could improve on her style.'

It is the style of intelligent, concerned speech. Read it out aloud and you will see how natural it is:

There was a man servant left to keep the house with me, and we generally made a practice of locking the doors during the hours of service; but on that occasion, the weather was so warm and pleasant that I set them wide open; and to fulfil my engagement, as I knew who would be coming, I told my companion that the mistress wished very much for some oranges, and he must run over to the village and get a few, to be paid for on the morrow. He departed, and I went upstairs.

Mrs Linton sat in a loose, white dress, with a light shawl over her shoulders, in the recess of the open window, as usual. Her thick, long hair had been partly removed at the beginning of her illness; and now she wore it simply combed in its natural tresses over her temples and neck. Her appearance was altered, as I had told Heathcliff, but when she was calm there seemed unearthly beauty in the change (beginning of the chapter, pp. 155–6).

Notice how closely observed this is and how familiar it all seems. Nelly Dean's affectionate memory recalls everything and we believe her utterly. This is one of Emily Brontë's most important devices for securing credibility. The business with the oranges helps this. Notice too how the rhythm of the sentences is wholly natural. This is particularly true of the second paragraph. Here again the detail is beautifully observed, but notice how naturally it leads up to the last phrase and its effortless and convincing poetry. We have moved from the business of buying oranges to a beautiful woman on the edge of death. How easy Emily Brontë makes it seem!

If Nelly Dean's narrative is subtle, it is also various. She can describe high dramas in the short, jerky sentences she employs when recounting Heathcliff's reaction to Catherine's death (p. 167). She also has an expert command of verbal pace.

One of the great strengths of the novel is its dialogue. Joseph's is not easy to read but is convincing when mastered. It has the effect of permeating the whole book with its Yorkshire tang and though, probably, the others too would have talked with a strong accent (Nelly singles out Edgar for his less local voice) the provincial strain is still felt. It is helped from time to time by such colloquialisms as 'rough as a saw-edge, and hard as whinstone', or 'dree and dreary!'

But it is in the great speeches that we hear the voice of the poet, of the writer capable of high, unpompous emotion. Catherine's confession of her love for Heathcliff and perhaps even more his outburst to her (pp. 160–61) are fine examples. Every adjective here is bitterly relished, every emphasis a blow and every parenthesis a wince.

Given this degree of authenticity it is appropriate that the otherwise rather passive Lockwood should be sufficiently moved by what he has heard to utter the sonorous cadences of the last paragraph of the book.

Structure

The structure of *Wuthering Heights* has been adversely criticized but is, in fact, well designed for Emily Brontë's purpose. The plot is, in addition, both dense and fast moving.

It is designed in three parts: Chapters 1–3 form the introduction, Chapters 4 (Volume I) to 16 (Volume II) make up Nelly Dean's narrative, and the last four chapters describe the affair of Hareton and Cathy. The long central section is lightly subdivided at the end of Chapter 7, Chapter 9 when Heathcliff has disappeared and Catherine and Edgar have married, after Chapter 14 to prepare us for the great scene that follows, after Chapter 3 (Volume II) when there is a twelve-year gap as the younger generation matures, and after Chapter 10 (Volume II) when we are within a year of Lockwood's arrival.

The subdivisions of the main section are natural and have the effect of reminding us that we are listening to a story, hearing it at second (or even sometimes third) hand. The divisions after Chapter 3 and Chapter 16 (Volume II), however, are more significant.

The first three chapters are a tone poem descriptive of the macabre. They are masterfully contrived. Bitterness and degradation are evident in them. The coarseness of moorland life and a feeling of repressed passion predominate. We are introduced to three of the main characters in such a way that we share Lockwood's embarrassment as he gets their very complicated relationship wrong. We want to find out the real relationship between them and also the reason for the gloomy atmosphere. But in Chapter 3 Emily Brontë takes matters a stage further. Her novel will be concerned with the perilous line between sanity and madness in passion, and she creates a precise equivalent of this in Lockwood's nightmarish experiences. Having convinced us of this state she then shows Heathcliff's appeal to Catherine's ghost. The tight-lipped misanthrope shows himself to be a man of feeling. And what feeling! We could not have been better prepared for an encounter with a man losing his reason.

The plotting of the central section, it should be noted, is wonderfully precise. There is a wholly appropriate ruthlessness about it, and economy and fatalism which are profoundly dramatic. All seems to work to cause and then conspire with Heathcliff's revenge. We see how his hope of love is destroyed and then how he can manipulate what is left to his own advantage. He uses everyone in his grasp: Hindley, Hareton, Isabella, Linton and Cathy. He seems assured of a bitter success. He seems set to win as completely here as he does when he gambles with Hindley.

But Heathcliff and hate are not completely in control. Love is a positive and vital force in the world – just. Almost unbelievably Cathy and Hareton fall in love. Simultaneously, Heathcliff's strength for destruction is sapped. It is here that the central section closes.

The last section contrasts directly with the first. Indeed, this is the strongest of the many contrasts in the book. In the place of ghosts and nightmares, snowstorms and hostility, we have sunlight, literacy and love. The point could not be better made. Emotional stalemate has been resolved into love and evil has faded. The juxtaposition is moving and also profoundly ironic. The Earnshaws and Lintons are united now that the alien force of evil has gone. Instead of being destroyed and left destitute, the two families are stronger and, eventually, they will be richer through the marriage of Cathy and Hareton. Goodness and love, the very opposite of what Heathcliff represented, triumph at last.

Love in *Wuthering Heights*

(a) *Romantic passion.* The seventeenth-century French writer La Roche-foucauld said that the symptoms of great love resemble those of great hatred. In *Wuthering Heights* these two emotions merge. The relationship between Heathcliff and Catherine is obsessive. It rises to such climaxes and leads to such cruelty that our response must finally be one of awe. We cannot wholly admire, we cannot wholly blame. Here is a force of nature: elemental and beyond such simple words as good and bad. It is amoral. Like a destructive storm it is both beautiful and brutal. Like a storm too, it is profoundly exciting and electric.

Being natural, such passions belong to the children of nature. The young friendship of Catherine and Heathcliff is nurtured on the moors and as they mature the moors provide imagery for their love (see p. 82). Catherine identifies herself with Heathcliff and Heathcliff with the natural world. Throughout the novel the moors and the natural world provide the background for love and, when things go badly, a sort of wild consolation.

But for all that this is a novel of passion, Emily Brontë is never explicit about sex. Despite their ardour, there is no suggestion that Catherine and Heathcliff have slept with each other. The conventions of the time forbade such a thought. Quite simply, Heathcliff and Catherine were not married. It is idle to ask how Emily Brontë might have written her novel in our day. Far better to accept the fact that Heathcliff and Catherine have not consummated their love and then see how Emily Brontë exploits the convention of silence on such things.

The excitement of the woman is clear all the way through, but when Catherine denies the possibility of marriage to Heathcliff she denies her sexual passion for him as well. This drives Heathcliff away and the effect on him (desire for revenge) and the effect on her (nervous collapse when he returns) says much about the nature of passion. Repressed passion destroys. The longings of the body and soul turn in on the mind. Joy thwarted turns sour, and nature, when denied, destroys its own (see pp. 160–61).

This connection between grand passion and death is important. It is Catherine's denying of her passion that forges the terrible link. Because she has denied the meaning of her life, she must die. Before this last scene her thoughts have already run on death (p. 126). Now she has a hysterical certainty: 'No!' she shrieked. 'Oh, don't, don't go. It is the last time! Edgar will not hurt us. Heathcliff, I shall die! I shall die!' (p. 162). Her anguish, in his presence, leads to her death.

Nelly Dean rounds on Heathcliff and declares: 'That is the most diabolical deed that you ever did.'

And we must recognize that the diabolic, the mysteriously evil part of Heathcliff, is an essential part of this affair. The physical traces of the devil in him are often mentioned (pp. 36, 56, 95, 326). The natural world of the moors from which the love of Heathcliff and Catherine derives is not always good. Its violent weather can cause fevers and kill. It can nurture Heathcliff. Catherine herself is perfectly well aware of the evil in Heathcliff. The vastness of their love includes a recognition of evil. But the natural savage in Heathcliff is perhaps most clear when Nelly Dean tells him of Catherine's death (see p. 167). After his death

Nelly Dean thinks about his possible connections with the devil.

The devil in Heathcliff shows when he is denied fulfilment of his love. The second half of the novel is concerned with how such love, when turned to bitterness and frustration, perverts its energies to destruction. Nonetheless, the destructive Heathcliff remains an awe-inspiring figure. Not only is his revenge fascinating in its ruthlessness, but Emily Brontë also manages to win for him a measure of sympathy. The devil has the upper hand, but Heathcliff is a soul in pain. Set against his bitter, fruitless revenge is the unforgettable picture of Heathcliff sobbing to Catherine's ghost. Throughout the second half of the novel and while we are watching Heathcliff, the destroyer, we are also presented with the soul in anguish. You should compare what we learn of him in Chapter 13 with how this is modified in Chapter 14. Again, near the end of the book (p. 321) Heathcliff admits to Nelly Dean the pain he is suffering. Love frustrated has given its energies to evil. Nonetheless, something of extreme and pathetic ardour remains. The haunted Heathcliff, a soul in pain and punishment, is at once profoundly pathetic and sinister. To see this, you should compare different descriptions of him (pp. 28–9, 286–7). As Lockwood looks on their graves and thinks of the bodies of Catherine and Heathcliff merging into one dust we may, with him, think they are at peace. On the other hand we may share the opinion of some of the locals and imagine that the spirit of this sinister man, once filled with romantic passion, then with the will to destroy, and finally with longing for his lover's ghost, can indeed find no rest but still haunts the local people.

(b) *Married love*. Reluctantly, Lockwood recognizes the strength and purity of Cathy's and Hareton's love: "*They* are afraid of nothing," I grumbled, watching their approach through the window. "Together they would brave satan and all his legions." And, in a sense they have done. They have braved Heathcliff and won.

Though perhaps not as compelling or convincing as the love of Heathcliff and Catherine, the love of Cathy and Hareton offers, at the close of *Wuthering Heights*, more than a conventional 'happy ending'. It is Emily Brontë's statement that love does in the end triumph.

The sort of love that triumphs is happy and affectionate. We would apply no such adjectives to the relationship between Heathcliff and Catherine. Their love is neither caring nor positive. It leads to no redemption from brutality. Its images are of storm and rock. The love that finally emerges between Cathy and Hareton is very different. Lockwood's description of the couple when he first sees their redeemed state is the best expression of this (pp. 304–5). The couple are reading together affectionately. Cathy offers Hareton primroses and together they build a garden. The wild storm-tossed moors are quietened and the natural, delicate images express the love of Cathy and Hareton. A garden is nature tamed, made civilized.

This state has not come about easily. Hareton has been all but wrecked by Heathcliff and Heathcliff has taken a delight in this because of Hareton's potential for good.

Heathcliff believes that his power of evil can eliminate all. He believes that natural evil is stronger than innate goodness, but he is wrong and it is important that we recognize this.

Cathy too, though she has a great ability to love, at first despises Hareton and is cruel to him. Her goodness too is all but destroyed by Heathcliff. But the sullen Cathy we meet at the start of the novel is not the true one. Her innate goodness, encouraged by Nelly Dean, eventually surfaces and, prompted by conscience, she begins to work the redemption of Hareton. We have been hoping for this since we first saw his efforts to improve himself. These efforts were, of course, greatly encouraged by Cathy's beauty.

But Emily Brontë is too strong a writer to let the affair between Cathy and Hareton appear either easy or oversentimental. Partly for the sake of contrast which, as we have seen, is a vital part of her technique, the relationship between Cathy and Hareton is as remote as it could possibly be from the happiness with which we are finally presented. We first see Cathy in love with Linton. This is not a healthy or particularly happy business and finally we must be glad that it never really establishes itself. The sort of happy love that Emily Brontë was concerned to show was that between two strong, healthy people. Linton is neither. He is sickly and peevish. He recognizes a certain need for Cathy's affection, but the real motivation behind him is his fear of his father and Heathcliff's overwhelming ambition to destroy the enemies of his childhood by gaining possession of Thrushcross Grange. Nonetheless, the relationship as it is portrayed does serve to show the great care that Cathy is capable of lavishing on those less fortunate than herself. Nelly Dean makes a point of describing her care for others as a young girl. Cathy is not like her mother. Her emotions do not naturally stretch to a wild extreme. She has within her an ability to care which will be so marked at the end of the book when it has indeed found a worthy object.

It is under Linton's baleful influence that she develops her initial dislike for Hareton. She is horrified at the thought that he is her cousin because she is repelled by his baseness. Heathcliff's unnatural influence is explained to her and, while she can learn to be horrified at Heathcliff and to realize the depth of hatred in his loveless life, it takes some time to see what her real duty is towards Hareton.

Heathcliff himself cannot see this and he is so confident of his destructive powers that he cannot imagine that Cathy will ever redeem the brutal Hareton. He has eliminated conscience from his life and it is through the lack of this that he can act as he does. But Emily Brontë is concerned to show that people cannot successfully live in this way. She is concerned to show that conscience has indeed a very important role in everyone's life. It is Nelly Dean's appeal to Cathy's conscience that eventually brings her round to considering Hareton in a more favourable light.

But the process is neither simple nor straightforward. The redemption through love that marks the conclusion of the novel was something that Emily Brontë wanted to present in the most dramatic way possible. She needed to show that Heathcliff does very nearly succeed in bringing about the destruction he desired. He comes very close indeed to reducing Cathy to the brutish level of his other victims.

And it is the sulking, unsociable Cathy that we meet at the start of the novel. This is yet another of the devices of contrast that Emily Brontë uses to bring diversity and drama to her book. Like Lockwood, we are fascinated and slightly repelled by this woman, and we are made to realize that there is something wrong, something missing. What Cathy needs, of course, is love. This is what she eventually learns to win.

Love is a powerful force. Emily Brontë contrasts its growth with the decline of Heathcliff's strength. Warily, Cathy makes her approaches to Hareton and slowly and painfully he begins to rise to the dignity of which he is capable. While it is important to realize that both of these young people have experienced very real degradation at the hands of Heathcliff, it is also important to see that they are stronger than he. As his vision of the ghostly Catherine becomes more powerful, more obsessive, so the love of Cathy and Hareton increases. As Heathcliff is driven nearer to the death that will at last free him from the earthly pain of the past eighteen years, so the younger generation advance to the life and married love that will be the final undoing of Heathcliff's long-meditated revenge. They plant a garden and are prepared to defend their action against his anger. They are taming nature rather than allowing themselves to be destroyed by its extreme manifestations. Hareton, it should be noted, forever stands in awe of Heathcliff and, in his primitive way, has a loyalty towards him that is touchingly expressed at his funeral. Nonetheless, we are shown a declining Heathcliff, a man whose will to destroy is being sapped by the growing demands of the cruel ghost of Catherine. He could oppose the love of Cathy and Hareton but he lacks the will. The vengeful hate of frustrated extremes of passion cannot resist true love and eventually works its own destruction.

With the death of Heathcliff, the way is clear for the relationship between Cathy and Hareton to ripen into the love clear in the charming domestic scene that Lockwood encounters on his return. The domestic aspect is important. Just as Cathy and Hareton plant a garden at the beginning of their love, so affection grows and turns naturally to thoughts of marriage and the future. Neither are simply sweet and innocent characters. Both, particularly Hareton, have suffered appallingly. But their love, when they find it, is strong. It can undo all of the planning that Heathcliff has so long treasured. They can unite in love and peace. In so doing they can unite the houses that Heathcliff spent eighteen years trying to tear apart.

The Nature of Evil

This leads us naturally to sum up what we have said about Emily Brontë's portrayal of evil in *Wuthering Heights.*

She does not try to trace the origin of evil. We can say, of course, that it comes from Heathcliff. But where does he come from? No one ever finds out. He is a strange, swarthy child whom a kind old man adopts and whose family he wrecks. Nelly Dean wonders where Heathcliff comes from (p. 360) but she can find no satisfactory answer. Throughout, Heathcliff is marked by his evil nature. It is clear in his face as a boy and it is stressed when he returns a rich man. Money and the trappings of a gentleman can do nothing to remove what nature has given him. Emily Brontë is wonderfully subtle in her presentation of Heathcliff. Heathcliff is a thoroughly ambiguous and enigmatic character: as a child he has a wonderful sense of love and freedom but as a man he is a destroyer. If he is a destroyer, he is also a pain-racked soul. He becomes hideously worldly yet he has a poet's vision of Catherine's ghost. We are shown by his treatment of Isabella that he can abuse love in the most heartless fashion. But we cannot say that Heathcliff has no heart. So great are the passions in him that they can only inspire awe.

His greatness as a boy and as a young man is his ability to love. This, as we have said, comes from his naturalness, his love of freedom, his lack of inhibition. He is cruelly betrayed. All that is most valuable, all that gives his life meaning, is sold for security. Heathcliff's vast energies are denied joy and turn to evil. Evil, for Emily Brontë, is the will to destroy. Heathcliff is magnificent at this. He destroys Hindley and comes very close to destroying Cathy. In a wonderful chapter (Chapter 15) his presence brings about the collapse and death of a woman who has destroyed both of them.

And we should be careful not to lay the whole blame at Heathcliff's feet. When Catherine denied him, when she denied the love that gave meaning to her whole life, she too did wrong. Heathcliff was her soul and she knew he was. When she denied him she denied her soul. For that she suffers and dies.

Heathcliff's revenge is in terrible proportion. He wants to destroy the whole world in which he was humiliated as a boy and denied love as a man. The way the plot is constructed, the way that Heathcliff takes advantage of the situation to level all before him, is both compelling and revolting. And yet the ambiguity remains. He is still the great lover, the man haunted by Catherine's cruel ghost.

But although this force of evil seems to triumph, although all the most important cards seem to come to his hand, in the end Heathcliff is destroyed and evil is destroyed. Evil cannot, finally, keep its momentum to fulfil itself. Heathcliff cannot, in the end, master the strength of goodness. His remembered love becomes ever more insistent and his will to ruin weaker. Evil, in the last resort, is self-destructive and its failing forces are routed by love, by Cathy and Hareton. What Heathcliff's evil had most desired – the destruction of the Earnshaw and Linton houses – is not achieved. They are united in a love stronger than evil.

Depravity and Brutishness

When Nelly Dean informs Heathcliff of Catherine's death (p. 166) the primitive animal emerges. Yet there is something both pathetic and terrible in the slaughter of a noble beast. Likewise, there is something terrible in Heathcliff's anguish. Even at this moment he is awesome.

With the other characters this is not the case; they sink to the level of animals but without any nobility. They are not exciting but they are depressing.

Hindley is the first to succumb to the extreme pressures. After the death of his wife he seeks consolation in drink, and rapidly becomes an alcoholic. He is unable to preserve any of the veneer of civilization that so lightly covers the characters in the book. He allows his son to decline to the same level. When he realizes that his gambling has almost ruined him and that Wuthering Heights has fallen into the hands of his boyhood enemy, he tries pathetically to get his revenge. We have seen him, in his vicious state, try to murder Hareton (p. 74) and we have seen the cruel irony by which the child is saved by Heathcliff.

When both characters are in the grip of the mature Heathcliff, Hindley tries to murder him. His revenge is impotent and pathetic and he is eventually kicked to death by the man he wanted to kill.

The latter part of Hindley Earnshaw's life and the boyhood of his son make, intentionally, depressing reading. Emily Brontë wanted to show that the unpleasant, the vicious, all the destructive things in men, lie very close to the surface. The world of emotions is, in her view, a perilous one and is both ruthless and destructive. In this wild place on the moors and among these people, civilization is easily threatened. Those who threaten to destroy it also destroy themselves.

How few people in the book are shown reading! Nelly Dean can read and she commands our respect throughout. Cathy reads and it is through her reading that she civilizes Hareton. With Cathy's love come such good things as gardens and books. They are sustained by her love for Hareton. Joseph can read but cannot love. He too wallows at the animal level of those deprived of love.

It is highly significant that when Lockwood returns to Wuthering Heights, to a world of caring love, the first thing he sees at the house is a young couple reading. Love overcomes the bestial in man and is stronger than evil.

Critical and Historical Notes

Critics have used a number of words and expressions you may find useful when writing essays. Though some of these words may at first seem difficult, they are an efficient way of explaining ideas. Here are some you may find convenient.

pathetic fallacy: this is when a writer assumes that nature (either weather or the landscape) is like the moods of his characters. This idea is central to *Wuthering Heights*. The wild, uncivilized moors are like the wild, uncivilized people. When Catherine has declared that she loves Heathcliff but will not marry him, she runs out into a storm (p. 84). This storm is like her own passion: untameable and dangerous. But the moors are not only destructive. They can be cleared for a garden and primroses grow there. Cathy gives these flowers to the redeemed Hareton. The moors can mirror tempestuous love; they can also reflect gentle love. When she presents the moors in harmony with her characters, Emily Brontë is using the pathetic fallacy.

ambiguous: when something is ambiguous it suggests a lack of clarity. This is not always a fault. Emily Brontë's treatment of Heathcliff is ambiguous: we are sympathetic to him and horrified by him. Both these feelings are right and true. We can never finally make up our minds about him. Emily Brontë uses ambiguity to make Heathcliff complex and lifelike.

romantic: we call Emily Brontë a 'romantic' writer. This is not because she is telling a love story, a 'romance'. It is because, like many artists of her age, she put feelings first. Critics call such writers, painters and musicians of the period 'romantic'. Because *Wuthering Heights* is concerned above all with feeling it is a romantic novel, and Emily Brontë is a romantic writer.

idiomatic or *colloquial speech:* none of us speaks all of the time in the manner of a well-written essay. We use slang and our accent shows our background. Emily Brontë is careful to give Joseph idiomatic or colloquial speech so that she can give us a feeling for a particular part of the country, in this case Yorkshire.

flashback: most of *Wuthering Heights* is told through a series of flash-backs. We are presented with something that is happening in the present tense such as the life that Lockwood sees at Wuthering Heights when he first arrives, or the improved life he finds when he returns; we then go back in time to be told how these ways of life came about.

didactic: this word concerns those parts of the novel which offer a message. Emily Brontë has important things to say about the nature of love, but her approach is not heavily didactic. In other words, she does not preach her ideas in a crude, obvious way.

Times change and with them people's way of life. What Emily Brontë thought of as normal we may find strange. A few of these points are outlined below.

servants: few of us now keep servants and so it is important to recognize that a servant was not always a despised menial there to be ordered about. A good servant was a respected member of a household and in some cases almost one of the family. Respected servants, like Nelly Dean, had considerable influence and responsibility.

the place of children: the treatment of children in *Wuthering Heights* is sterner and more protective than is normal today. The treatment of Heathcliff and Catherine at the hands of Joseph is excessive, but you should note how young Cathy is protected by her father, not being allowed out of the grounds of Thrushcross Grange all of the time she is a child. More authoritarian attitudes than we are used to today were quite normal at the time. They do not necessarily imply a lack of love.

isolated communities: greater communications have made communities as isolated as those in this book unusual today. Lockwood is very much a stranger in a place where the ways of life are different from those he is familiar with. You should note how the isolation draws the characters together and how this heightens the drama.

property ownership: this was far more significant in the past and in the isolated countryside where owning a farm meant real power. Heathcliff wants this power to get his revenge. It is why he is so ruthless in his pursuit of the ownership of both Wuthering Heights and Thrushcross Grange. The laws on inheritance helped him here.

inheritance of money and land by women: this is important to the novel since Heathcliff's plans to win for himself the right to control Thrushcross Grange depend on the fact that Edgar's heirs are both women: his sister Isabella and his daughter Cathy. In general, the property of a married woman belonged to her husband. This seems very unfair to us nowadays and the law has now been changed. However, to Heathcliff, this fact was a vital one. Should Isabella have been left any rights in Thrushcross Grange by Edgar, Heathcliff already controlled these as her husband. Should, as is most likely, Edgar have left half or all of the property to his daughter, it was vital that Heathcliff get control of it by marrying his son to her. It was also vital that Edgar should not change his will in such a way that the property was left to Cathy in her own right. He could do this. This was why he summoned Green, the lawyer, and why Heathcliff had to delay him. It is part of Heathcliff's revenge that he presents the forced marriage of his son Linton and the young Cathy to the girl's father when it is too late for the dying Edgar to do anything. Helpless, he sees his child and his land become Heathcliff's property.

Glossary

Agait: afoot
Ague: feverish fit
Allwildered like: looking
    bewildered
An: if
Aw daht: I'm afraid
Bahn: going
Baht: without
Bairn: child
Banning: swearing
Beaver: beaver fur hat
Beck: stream
Bespeak: ask for
Blubbering: crying
Bog hoile: hole in the marsh
Bout: without
Brach: bitch
Brass: money
Brown study: deep thought
Brusts: bursts
Cambric: linen
Cant: brisk
Changeling: a baby secretly
    swapped for another
Childer: children
Chit: girl
Chuck: dear

Cipher: a nondescript person
Clothes-press: wardrobe
Clown: peasant
Cockatrice: an imaginary reptile
Conned: learned
Copestone: i.e. finishing touch
Coxcomb: fool
Crahnr's quest enah: coroner's
    inquest enough
Devastate the moors: a shooting
    party
Diurnal: daily
Dree: joyless
Dunnock: hedge sparrow. The
    cuckoo uses other birds'
    nests for its own.
Een: eyes
Eft: small lizard
Elder: senior lay person
Elf-bolt: i.e. a flint arrowhead
Elysium: the ancient Greek
    Heaven, i.e. perfect
    happiness
Fahl: foul
Fairishes: fairies
Fellies: fellows
Fit: feet

Flags: flagstones
Flaysome: terrifying
Flighted: scolded
Flitting: moving
Foreigners: any strangers
Frame: go quickly
Frame: invent
Galloway: small horse
Ganging: going
Gaumless: stupid
Gentle: well born
Ghoul: a grave-robbing spirit
Girn: snarl
Glees: songs
Grat: wept
Grimalkin: a name for a cat
    perhaps deriving from
    Macbeth
Habit: riding dress
Hahs: house
Hahsomidiver: however
Harried: carried
Heath: heather
Hemmed: to make a 'hem' sound
Hend: hand
Hives, stand of: structure for
    placing beehives on
Humour: mood
Indigenae: local people
Jocks: provisions
Laced: thrashed
Laiking: playing
Laith: born
Lantern jaws: long, thin jaws
Lascar: East Indian sailor
Lath: weakling

Lay: forget
Lees: fields for grazing
Likker: likely
Ling: heather
Lugs: ears
Madling: foolish person
Mattock: used for loosening
    hard ground
Maxillary: of the jaw
Meeterly clane: clear enough
Mell on't: interferes with
Mensful: clean
Mitch: lucky
Mitch: much
Mim: prim
Misanthropist: one who hates the
    world
Mither: mother
Monomania: mad concerning
    one thing
Mools, beneath the: under the
    earth
Mulled: mixed with sugar and
    spice and warmed
Mummy: mush
Neeght: night
Negus: warmed wine and water
'Never told my love': an adapted
    quotation from *Twelfh
    Night*
Noah and Lot: Old Testament
    figures saved from
    destruction by God
Norther: neither
Nowt: good for nothing
Orther: either

Ousel: small, thrush-like bird
Overdone: overcome
Parte t' guilp: skim off froth
Penetralium: humorous word for innermost parts
Phalanx of vials: row of bottles
Pharisee: hypocrite
Pikes: turnpike gates
Pining: starring
Plottered: floundered
Preterhuman: beyond human powers
Quean: girl
Reaming: foaming
Riven: pulled
Rullers: rulers
Rush of a lass: slip of a girl
Sackless: weak
Sarve ye aht: get his own back on you
Say: see
Set: plant
Shameless: not ashamed of their nakedness
Shoon: shoes
Shou: she
Signet: personal mark i.e. hit him
Simple: ordinary person
Sizar: a Cambridge undergraduate who received tuition in return for services

Slop: invalid's food
Slough of Despond: total despair. From Bunyan's *Pilgrim's Progress*
Snoozled: nuzzled
Snuffed: trimmed
Sotto voce: whispered
Sough: ditch
Spleen: bad tempered
Springer: a kind of spaniel
Stalled at: fed up with
Stark: stiff
Strike my colours: surrender
Swells: ridges
Taen tent: taken care
Thrang: busy
Throstles: thrushes
Train oil: whale oil used for cleaning guns
Underbred pride: pride at being thought an ordinary working man
Underdrawn: the rafters were uncovered
Unlikely: unsuitable
Valances: drapery
Vis-à-vis: face to face
War on war: worse and worse
Wer: our
Wick: lively
Wicket: gate
Win: reach
Wisht: be quiet

Discussion Topics and Examination Questions

Your understanding and appreciation of the novel will be much increased if you discuss aspects of it with other people. Here are some topics you could consider:

1. Does the fact that so much about Heathcliff's origin is unexplained add to or detract from the force of the novel?
2. What do the remoteness and loneliness of the setting contribute to the effect of *Wuthering Heights*?
3. Grand romantic passion, such as that displayed in the novel, no longer impresses us. Do you agree or disagree?
4. Is our appreciation of this novel helped or hindered by everything in it seeming to be 'larger than life'?
5. What do you think of Emily Brontë's device of using Edward Lockwood and Nelly Dean to present the story?
6. Heathcliff is a most powerful and impressive character, but is he convincing as a human being?
7. Why does the love of Heathcliff and Catherine lead to destruction, whereas that of Cathy and Hareton promises future happiness?

The Examination

You may find that the set texts chosen by your teacher have been selected from a very wide list of suggestions in the examination syllabus. The questions in the examination paper will therefore be applicable to many different books. Here are some questions which you could answer by making use of *Wuthering Heights*:

1. Write about a book you know in which a leading character achieves his or her ambitions but finds no satisfaction in the achievement. Explain why this is so.

2. Choose a book in which the weather plays an important part and show how it *either* affects the development of the story *or* is used by the author to create atmosphere.

3. Select an episode from a book you know in which an overheard conversation is a significant feature. Outline the episode and show why it is important in the story.

4. Explore the nature and the quality of love between two contrasting couples in a book of your choice.

5. An evil character who is also desperately unhappy – write about such a person you have met in a novel.

6. Childhood experiences often profoundly affect adult life. Illustrate this from a book you know.

7. The fiercest passions often involve just one or two families. Select a book which uses this situation and discuss what evokes such passions.

Examination Questions on *Wuthering Heights*

1. Explain why Catherine married Edgar Linton despite her deep feelings for Heathcliff.

2. How important in this novel are class distinctions? Show their effect on one or more of the characters.

3. At the end of the novel, what are your feelings about Heathcliff?

4. Discuss the ways in which Thrushcross Grange presents a contrast to Wuthering Heights and show the use the author makes of this contrast in the novel.

5. Apart from being a narrator, what role does Nelly Dean play in the story?

6. Show how Emily Brontë uses the countryside in which her characters live as an important element in creating atmosphere.

PENGUIN ✺ CLASSICS

www.penguinclassics.com

- Details about every Penguin Classic

- Advanced information about forthcoming titles

- Hundreds of author biographies

- FREE resources including critical essays on the books and their historical background, reader's and teacher's guides.

- Links to other web resources for the Classics

- Discussion area

- Online review copy ordering for academics

- Competitions with prizes, and challenging Classics trivia quizzes

READ MORE IN PENGUIN

In every corner of the world, on every subject under the sun, Penguin represents quality and variety – the very best in publishing today.

For complete information about books available from Penguin – including Puffins, Penguin Classics and Arkana – and how to order them, write to us at the appropriate address below. Please note that for copyright reasons the selection of books varies from country to country.

In the United Kingdom: Please write to *Dept. EP, Penguin Books Ltd, Bath Road, Harmondsworth, West Drayton, Middlesex UB7 ODA*

In the United States: Please write to *Consumer Sales, Penguin Putnam Inc., P.O. Box 12289 Dept. B, Newark, New Jersey 07101-5289.* VISA and MasterCard holders call 1-800-788-6262 to order Penguin titles

In Canada: Please write to *Penguin Books Canada Ltd, 10 Alcorn Avenue, Suite 300, Toronto, Ontario M4V 3B2*

In Australia: Please write to *Penguin Books Australia Ltd, P.O. Box 257, Ringwood, Victoria 3134*

In New Zealand: Please write to *Penguin Books (NZ) Ltd, Private Bag 102902, North Shore Mail Centre, Auckland 10*

In India: Please write to *Penguin Books India Pvt Ltd, 11 Community Centre, Panchsheel Park, New Delhi 110017*

In the Netherlands: Please write to *Penguin Books Netherlands bv, Postbus 3507, NL-1001 AH Amsterdam*

In Germany: Please write to *Penguin Books Deutschland GmbH, Metzlerstrasse 26, 60594 Frankfurt am Main*

In Spain: Please write to *Penguin Books S. A., Bravo Murillo 19, 1° B, 28015 Madrid*

In Italy: Please write to *Penguin Italia s.r.l., Via Benedetto Croce 2, 20094 Corsico, Milano*

In France: Please write to *Penguin France, Le Carré Wilson, 62 rue Benjamin Baillaud, 31500 Toulouse*

In Japan: Please write to *Penguin Books Japan Ltd, Kaneko Building, 2-3-25 Koraku, Bunkyo-Ku, Tokyo 112*

In South Africa: Please write to *Penguin Books South Africa (Pty) Ltd, Private Bag X14, Parkview, 2122 Johannesburg*

PENGUIN AUDIOBOOKS

A Quality of Writing That Speaks for Itself

Penguin Books has always led the field in quality publishing. Now you can listen at leisure to your favourite books, read to you by familiar voices from radio, stage and screen. Penguin Audiobooks are produced to an excellent standard, and abridgements are always faithful to the original texts. From thrillers to classic literature, biography to humour, with a wealth of titles in between, Penguin Audiobooks offer you quality, entertainment and the chance to rediscover the pleasure of listening.

You can order Penguin Audiobooks through Penguin Direct by telephoning (0181) 899 4036. The lines are open 24 hours every day. Ask for Penguin Direct, quoting your credit card details.

A selection of Penguin Audiobooks, published or forthcoming:

Emma by Jane Austen, read by Fiona Shaw

Pride and Prejudice by Jane Austen, read by Joanna David

Beowulf translated by Michael Alexander, read by David Rintoul

Agnes Grey by Anne Brontë, read by Juliet Stevenson

Jane Eyre by Charlotte Brontë, read by Juliet Stevenson

Wuthering Heights by Emily Brontë, read by Juliet Stevenson

The Pilgrim's Progress by John Bunyan, read by David Suchet

The Moonstone by Wilkie Collins, read by Michael Pennington, Terrence Hardiman and Carole Boyd

Nostromo by Joseph Conrad, read by Michael Pennington

Tales from the Thousand and One Nights, read by Souad Faress and Raad Rawi

Robinson Crusoe by Daniel Defoe, read by Tom Baker

David Copperfield by Charles Dickens, read by Nathaniel Parker

Little Dorrit by Charles Dickens, read by Anton Lesser

Barnaby Rudge by Charles Dickens, read by Richard Pasco

The Adventures of Sherlock Holmes volumes 1–3 by Sir Arthur Conan Doyle, read by Douglas Wilmer

PENGUIN AUDIOBOOKS

The Man in the Iron Mask by Alexandre Dumas, read by Simon Ward

Adam Bede by George Eliot, read by Paul Copley

Joseph Andrews by Henry Fielding, read by Sean Barrett

The Great Gatsby by F. Scott Fitzgerald, read by Marcus D'Amico

North and South by Elizabeth Gaskell, read by Diana Quick

The Diary of a Nobody by George Grossmith, read by Terrence Hardiman

Jude the Obscure by Thomas Hardy, read by Samuel West

The Go-Between by L. P. Hartley, read by Tony Britton

Les Misérables by Victor Hugo, read by Nigel Anthony

A Passage to India by E. M. Forster, read by Tim Pigott-Smith

The Odyssey by Homer, read by Alex Jennings

The Portrait of a Lady by Henry James, read by Claire Bloom

On the Road by Jack Kerouac, read by David Carradine

Women in Love by D. H. Lawrence, read by Michael Maloney

Nineteen Eighty-Four by George Orwell, read by Timothy West

Ivanhoe by Sir Walter Scott, read by Ciaran Hinds

Frankenstein by Mary Shelley, read by Richard Pasco

Of Mice and Men by John Steinbeck, read by Gary Sinise

Dracula by Bram Stoker, read by Richard E. Grant

Gulliver's Travels by Jonathan Swift, read by Hugh Laurie

Vanity Fair by William Makepeace Thackeray, read by Robert Hardy

War and Peace by Leo Tolstoy, read by Bill Nighy

Barchester Towers by Anthony Trollope, read by David Timson

Tao Te Ching by Lao Tzu, read by Carole Boyd and John Rowe

Ethan Frome by Edith Wharton, read by Nathan Osgood

The Picture of Dorian Gray by Oscar Wilde, read by John Moffatt

Orlando by Virginia Woolf, read by Tilda Swinton

READ MORE IN PENGUIN

A CHOICE OF CLASSICS

Louisa May Alcott	**The Inheritance**
Kate Chopin	**The Awakening and Selected Stories**
James Fenimore Cooper	**The Deerslayer**
	The Last of the Mohicans
	The Pathfinder
	The Pioneers
	The Prairie
	The Spy
Stephen Crane	**The Red Badge of Courage**
Frederick Douglass	**Narrative of the Life of Frederick Douglass, An American Slave**
Nathaniel Hawthorne	**The Blithedale Romance**
	The House of the Seven Gables
	The Marble Faun
	The Scarlet Letter and Selected Tales
	Selected Tales and Sketches
Henry James	**The Ambassadors**
	The American Scene
	The Aspern Papers/The Turn of the Screw
	The Awkward Age
	The Bostonians
	The Critical Muse
	Daisy Miller
	The Europeans
	The Figure in the Carpet
	The Golden Bowl
	The Jolly Corner and Other Tales
	The Portrait of a Lady
	The Princess Casamassima
	Roderick Hudson
	The Sacred Fount
	The Spoils of Poynton
	The Tragic Muse
	Washington Square
	What Maisie Knew
	The Wings of the Dove

READ MORE IN PENGUIN

A CHOICE OF CLASSICS

Thomas Wentworth Higginson	**Army Life in a Black Regiment**
William Dean Howells	**The Rise of Silas Lapham**
Gilbert Imlay	**The Emigrants**
Sarah Orne Jewett	**The Country of the Pointed Firs**
Herman Melville	**Billy Budd, Sailor and Other Stories**
	The Confidence-Man
	Moby-Dick
	Pierre
	Redburn
	Typee
Thomas Paine	**Common Sense**
	The Rights of Man
	The Thomas Paine Reader
Edgar Allan Poe	**Comedies and Satires**
	The Fall of the House of Usher
	The Narrative of Arthur Gordon Pym of Nantucket
	The Science Fiction of Edgar Allan Poe
Jacob A. Riis	**How the Other Half Lives**
Elizabeth Stoddard	**The Morgesons**
Harriet Beecher Stowe	**Uncle Tom's Cabin**
Henry David Thoreau	**Walden/Civil Disobedience**
	Week on the Concord and Merrimack
Mark Twain	**The Adventures of Huckleberry Finn**
	The Adventures of Tom Sawyer
	A Connecticut Yankee at King Arthur's Court
	Life on the Mississippi
	The Prince and the Pauper
	Pudd'nhead Wilson
	Roughing It
	Short Stories
	A Tramp Abroad
	Tales, Speeches, Essays and Sketches
Walt Whitman	**The Complete Poems**
	Leaves of Grass

READ MORE IN PENGUIN

A CHOICE OF CLASSICS

Anton Chekhov	**The Duel and Other Stories**
	The Kiss and Other Stories
	The Fiancée and Other Stories
	Lady with Lapdog and Other Stories
	The Party and Other Stories
	Plays (The Cherry Orchard/Ivanov/The Seagull/Uncle Vania/The Bear/The Proposal/A Jubilee/Three Sisters)
Fyodor Dostoyevsky	**The Brothers Karamazov**
	Crime and Punishment
	The Devils
	The Gambler/Bobok/A Nasty Story
	The House of the Dead
	The Idiot
	Netochka Nezvanova
	The Village of Stepanchikovo
	Notes from Underground/The Double
Nikolai Gogol	**Dead Souls**
	Diary of a Madman and Other Stories
Alexander Pushkin	**Eugene Onegin**
	The Queen of Spades and Other Stories
	Tales of Belkin
Leo Tolstoy	**Anna Karenin**
	Childhood, Boyhood, Youth
	A Confession
	How Much Land Does a Man Need?
	Master and Man and Other Stories
	Resurrection
	The Sebastopol Sketches
	What is Art?
	War and Peace
Ivan Turgenev	**Fathers and Sons**
	First Love
	A Month in the Country
	On the Eve
	Rudin
	Sketches from a Hunter's Album

READ MORE IN PENGUIN

A CHOICE OF CLASSICS

Charles Dickens	**American Notes for General Circulation**
	Barnaby Rudge
	Bleak House
	The Christmas Books (in two volumes)
	David Copperfield
	Dombey and Son
	Great Expectations
	Hard Times
	Little Dorrit
	Martin Chuzzlewit
	The Mystery of Edwin Drood
	Nicholas Nickleby
	The Old Curiosity Shop
	Oliver Twist
	Our Mutual Friend
	The Pickwick Papers
	Pictures from Italy
	Selected Journalism 1850–1870
	Selected Short Fiction
	Sketches by Boz
	A Tale of Two Cities
George Eliot	**Adam Bede**
	Daniel Deronda
	Felix Holt
	Middlemarch
	The Mill on the Floss
	Romola
	Scenes of Clerical Life
	Silas Marner
Fanny Fern	**Ruth Hall**
Elizabeth Gaskell	**Cranford/Cousin Phillis**
	The Life of Charlotte Brontë
	Mary Barton
	North and South
	Ruth
	Sylvia's Lovers
	Wives and Daughters

READ MORE IN PENGUIN

A CHOICE OF CLASSICS

READ MORE IN PENGUIN

A CHOICE OF CLASSICS

Walter Scott	**The Antiquary**
	Heart of Mid-Lothian
	Ivanhoe
	Kenilworth
	The Tale of Old Mortality
	Rob Roy
	Waverley
Robert Louis Stevenson	**Kidnapped**
	Dr Jekyll and Mr Hyde and Other Stories
	In the South Seas
	The Master of Ballantrae
	Selected Poems
	Weir of Hermiston
William Makepeace Thackeray	**The History of Henry Esmond**
	The History of Pendennis
	The Newcomes
	Vanity Fair
Anthony Trollope	**Barchester Towers**
	Can You Forgive Her?
	Doctor Thorne
	The Eustace Diamonds
	Framley Parsonage
	He Knew He Was Right
	The Last Chronicle of Barset
	Phineas Finn
	The Prime Minister
	The Small House at Allington
	The Warden
	The Way We Live Now
Oscar Wilde	**Complete Short Fiction**
Mary Wollstonecraft	**A Vindication of the Rights of Woman**
	Mary and **Maria** (includes Mary Shelley's **Matilda**)
Dorothy and William Wordsworth	**Home at Grasmere**

READ MORE IN PENGUIN

A CHOICE OF CLASSICS

Matthew Arnold	**Selected Prose**
Jane Austen	**Emma**
	Lady Susan/The Watsons/Sanditon
	Mansfield Park
	Northanger Abbey
	Persuasion
	Pride and Prejudice
	Sense and Sensibility
William Barnes	**Selected Poems**
Mary Braddon	**Lady Audley's Secret**
Anne Brontë	**Agnes Grey**
	The Tenant of Wildfell Hall
Charlotte Brontë	**Jane Eyre**
	Juvenilia: 1829–35
	The Professor
	Shirley
	Villette
Emily Brontë	**Complete Poems**
	Wuthering Heights
Samuel Butler	**Erewhon**
	The Way of All Flesh
Lord Byron	**Don Juan**
	Selected Poems
Lewis Carroll	**Alice's Adventures in Wonderland**
	The Hunting of the Snark
Thomas Carlyle	**Selected Writings**
Arthur Hugh Clough	**Selected Poems**
Wilkie Collins	**Armadale**
	The Law and the Lady
	The Moonstone
	No Name
	The Woman in White
Charles Darwin	**The Origin of Species**
	Voyage of the Beagle
Benjamin Disraeli	**Coningsby**
	Sybil